God's Triumphant *Love*

Fall in Love With Jesus All Over Again!

Carol Zarska

TEACH Services, Inc.
P U B L I S H I N G
www.TEACHServices.com • (800) 367-1844

Copyright © Carol Zarska
Copyright © 2014 TEACH Services, Inc.
ISBN-13: 978-1-4796-0332-9 (Paperback)
ISBN-13: 978-1-4796-0332-6 (ePub)
ISBN-13: 978-1-4796-0334-3 (Mobi)
Library of Congress Control Number: 2014938922

Published by

TEACH Services, Inc.
PUBLISHING
www.TEACHServices.com • (800) 367-1844

About the Author

Carol Zarska has a master's degree in religion and pastoral counseling. She has been an avid student of end-time events for nearly fifty years and is widely known in Seventh-day Adventist church circles as "the Sanctuary Lady" because of a practical application of Old Testament sanctuary principles in current prayer life she developed that is now known as the sanctuary prayer.

Carol has been an American Christian Ministries speaker since 1984 with over 150 titles available. Her seminars have been recorded around the globe in places such as South Africa, Germany, Australia, Toronto, and the U.S. Through careful research and prayerful study, Carol's cutting edge messages focus on family healing and end-time events. They bring hope, encouragement, and focus to many people around the world.

Carol is still married to her high-school sweetheart, Ken. They have three grown children, a granddaughter, and two great-grandchildren. Carol and Ken live on a wooded mountaintop ninety minutes from Washington D.C. and Baltimore, Maryland. From her desk, Carol watches God's creatures scurry about preparing nests for their offspring, demonstrating God's matchless love for the least of His creations.

"I finished the book almost in one day, actually a few hours. It is incredible, and I can't wait to share it with all of my friends who I know are searching. This is what we needed! A way to help people (and myself) wrap their minds around the whole story and realize what Christ has done for them and what our lives really mean in the context of the universe and eternity. Amazing! I have a feeling this is message is going to be spreading like wildfire! I'm going to read it a few more times!"

Kathryn S.

"Your book is amazing! I cried, I prayed, I recommitted my life. I cannot imagine a world without such love. I don't think we even have the words to truly express God's love. I know I can't comprehend it."

Karen I.

"I have known Carol Zarska for many years and have attended many of her seminars. Finally, after much encouragement from her friends and family, she has written a wonderful book. She now has, in print, the passion of her heart and her life's work, which is to portray God's love for us coupled with an appeal to get closer to Him. I read *God's Triumphant Love* and was very moved by the smooth flow and heartfelt inspiration of her words, revealing the grand story of redemption in a beautiful and melodic manner. She concluded the book by outlining the Christian's role and mission on earth today. I believe God inspired this piece and blessed her efforts by painting this portrait with her. I believe many readers will feel the same and will be motivated to show our Precious Redeemer a greater love and commitment. I loved it!"

Meg S.

Table of Contents

Introduction vii

Prologue xi

Chapter 1   God's Original Blueprint 11

Chapter 2   Lucifer's Rebellion 18

Chapter 3   The Sacrifice 22

Chapter 4   The Plan 29

Chapter 5   The Creation 35

Chapter 6   The Fall 39

Chapter 7   The Covering 43

Chapter 8   The Sanctuary 48

Chapter 9   The Witness 51

Chapter 10   The Victory 57

Chapter 11   The Outpouring 62

Chapter 12   The Final Generation 67

Conclusion 81

Appendix 1   Christ's Heavenly Ministry 91

Appendix 2   Second Witnessing 103

Bibliography 105

Introduction

Over the thirty years of my public ministry, I have written enough material to fill several books. I have used my writings in a limited way to augment my seminars or to write down ideas that would come to my mind. But this time it was different. Day and night words, phrases, and scenes would tumble through my mind. I felt an urgency to capture on paper what I was experiencing so that it would not escape forever.

As the chapters gradually developed, I realized that this was the intimate story of Jesus, my Lord, from the time sin entered the courts of heaven, through His earthly journey, and culminating in His glorious second coming and triumphant return to heaven with His people. All the old, familiar stories I knew so well came alive once more; I felt that I was a part of the drama of Jesus' life. I was falling in love with Him in a way that I had never experienced before.

Writing this book has changed my life forever and I hope it will do the same for you. I pray that you, too, will fall in love with Jesus all over again!

Prologue

Forever from "His great and calm eternity, God has ruled over space and time" (White, *Testimonies for the Church*, vol. 8, p. 273). God is the divine embodiment of a mysterious character quality called "love." I say mysterious because no matter how many words are used to describe love, it can ultimately only be experienced or observed. No one can force love, create love, or explain its existence or origin. And that is because it exists only in the heart of God and those who receive it from Him. Oceans cannot contain it, poets and philosophers cannot describe it, and scientists cannot manufacture it. Love is the product of a relationship with God and the outpouring of Himself into everything that He has created.

Human love is but a faint reflection of God's love, because it has become so tainted and distorted by sin and selfishness, and intermingled with the attributes of Satan. The Devil uses this human need as his most effective trap to drag mankind into his web of passions of all types. But in His infinite foreknowledge, God saw the tragedy of the fall of man. Thus He prepared a plan, even before the creation of Adam and Eve, by which He would restore the human race to His original purpose for them—to be one with Him, and recipients of the fullness and unblemished perfection of His love. His plan of rescue was in place before the creation of the world. He would sacrifice His Son, the Beloved of His Bosom to become one with the fallen race, yet without sin, to display to the universe what love really looks like, and what the power of love can do to triumph over evil.

The purpose and goal of this book is to bring new light and hope to those who may be struggling with personal issues and un-answered questions, "to shine on those living in darkness and in the shadow of death, to guide our feet into the path of peace" (Luke 1:79). Jesus is coming soon—may this book help to prepare us to live His life of love until He comes.

Chapter 1

God's Original Blueprint

Love cannot exist without expression. For there to be love, there must be at least two beings—the lover and the beloved. And the love expressed by the lover must be accepted, validated, and returned back to the originator of the love exchange. So in the universe there are two Beings who follow this description to a perfection beyond the ability of even the greatest created mind to encompass. "All the paternal love which has come down from generation to generation through the channel of human hearts... are but a tiny rill to the boundless ocean when compared with the infinite, exhaustless love of God ... Yet there is an infinity beyond ... Eternity itself can never fully reveal it" (White, *The Faith I Live By*, p. 43).

At the nucleus of this love are the two divine Beings from whom radiates all life, and who are themselves the source of the power that love produces when ignited by divinity. Although we can never really understand these two sacred Beings, we have been created in their image and likeness, with the capacity and purpose of receiving their love and reproducing it in the families of earth. In order to do this, we must get to know them personally and intimately through the relationship made possible by the third person of the Godhead, the Holy Spirit. Without a body, He interacts with both members of the Godhead, and as their representative He extends throughout the created universe to bring the power and presence of the Father and His Son into everything that has life. He especially fills the heart of every person who desires an intimate relationship with Him, as is demonstrated in the following texts.

> From the throne came flashes of lightning, rumblings and peals of thunder. In front of the throne, seven lamps were blazing. These are the seven Spirits of God. (Rev. 4:5)

> Then I saw a Lamb, looking as if it had been slain, standing in the center of the throne... The Lamb had seven horns and seven eyes, which are the seven spirits of God sent out into all the earth. (Rev. 5:6)

> For the eyes of the Lord range throughout the earth to strengthen those whose hearts are fully committed to him. (2 Chron. 16:9)

> Those controlled by the sinful nature cannot please God. You, however, are controlled not by the sinful nature but by the Spirit, if the Spirit of God lives in you. And if anyone does not have the Spirit of Christ, he does not belong to Christ.... And if the Spirit of Him who raised Jesus from the dead is living in you, He who raised Christ from the dead will also give life to your mortal bodies through His Spirit, who lives in you. (Rom. 8:8–11)

So let's become better acquainted with these divine beings that are longing to share their most intimate thoughts and emotions with us and to reproduce themselves in every person who is willing to receive them into their hearts and lives.

First, let us behold the Father, the eternal powerhouse of the universe, the One who has inhabited eternity forever, and from whom all life and being flows. In Daniel 7:9, 13, 22, He is called the "Ancient of Days." In Aramaic, this is a title of veneration and honor emphasizing wisdom and power. As used in various other Old Testament texts, the word "ancient" means: everlasting, forever, eternal, never again, permanent, endless, life. He is "the Creator of all worlds... the great Source of all... the great Giver, the law of life" (White, *The Desire of Ages*, p. 21).

But God the Father is not alone in His work of beneficence for the creatures that He has created. He has a counterpart—another divine Being like Himself, who is called His beloved Son. He, too, is eternal, and has all the powers of His Father. He is so much like His Father that they function as one. And yet, there is a difference between the two. No one can really comprehend this sameness and yet difference, but we can get glimpses of this mystery through what they have chosen to reveal through the Bible and the Spirit of Prophecy.

> In the beginning was the Word, and the Word was with God, and the Word was God. He was with God in the beginning. Through him all things were made; without him nothing was made that has been made. In him was life, and that life was the light of mankind... The Word became flesh and made his dwelling among us. We have seen his glory, the glory of the one and only Son [mg. Only Begotten], who came from the Father, full of grace and truth... No one has ever seen God, but the one and only Son [mg. Only Begotten Son], who is himself God and is in closest relationship with the Father, has made him known. (John 1:1–4, 14, 18)

In Greek, the phrase, "Only Begotten," are comprehended in just one word—*monogenes*, meaning: only born, sole, only begotten child. But this word has fascinating implications in light of today's scientific understanding of the word, *genes*. From my medical dictionary I read this definition: "A factor present in the gametes which is responsible for the transmission of hereditary characteristics to the offspring" (*Taber's Cyclopedic Medical Dictionary*, p. 13). And according to my well-worn dictionary, the prefix, "mono-" means: alone, single, only. Although we cannot equate the eternal co-existence of God the Father and His Son with human parenting which has a beginning and an end, the use of "monogenes" would seem to indicate that Jesus, God's precious, beloved and only Son, is an exact duplicate of the Father. He has the same character, the same powers, the same abilities, and the same nature.

> Christ, the Word, the only begotten of God, was one with the eternal Father—one in nature, in character, in purpose. (White, *Patriarchs and Prophets*, p. 34).

> He and the Father were of one substance. (White, "The True Sheep Respond to the Voice of the Shepherd," *The Signs of the Times,* November 27, 1893)

> The Son is the radiance of God's glory and the exact representation of His being. (Heb. 1:3)

> Looking upon Christ in humanity, we look upon God, and see in him the brightness of his glory, the express image of his person. (White, "Child Life of Jesus," *The Signs of the Times,* July 30, 1896)

> From the days of eternity the Lord Jesus Christ

was one with the Father; He was 'the image of God,' the image of His greatness and majesty, 'the out shining of His glory.'" (White, *The Desire of Ages*, p. 19)

Christ, the Word, the only begotten of God, was one with the eternal Father,—one in nature, in character, in purpose,— the only being that could enter into all the counsels and purposes of God.... And the Son of God declares concerning Himself: 'The Lord possessed me in the beginning of His way, before His works of old. I was set up from everlasting.... When He appointed the foundations of the earth, then I was by Him, as one brought up with Him; and I was daily His delight, rejoicing always before Him (Prov. 8:22–30).'" (Ibid., p. 34)

Yet for all of this, there has always been a difference in role and function between the Father and the Son from eternity. It is this very difference that caused the beginning of the sin of envy and jealousy that originated in the heart of Lucifer. He questioned why Jesus was exalted above himself. This difference was certainly not in appearance, character or power, but in the perception that Lucifer had of the position of God's Son. "The exaltation of the Son of God as equal with the Father was represented as an injustice to Lucifer, who, it was claimed, was also entitled to reverence and honor" (White, *Patriarchs and Prophets*, p. 37).

In response to this challenge to the position of Christ in the Godhead is presented in the following passage.

The King of the universe summoned the heavenly hosts before Him, that in their presence He might set forth the true position of His Son, and

show the relation He sustained to all created beings. The Son of God shared the Father's throne,
and the glory of the eternal, self-existent One encircled both.... Before the assembled inhabitants
of heaven, the King declared that none but Christ,
the Only Begotten of God, could fully enter into
His purposes, and to Him it was committed to execute the mighty counsels of His will. The Son of
God had wrought the Father's will in the creation
of all the hosts of heaven; and to Him, as well as
to God, their homage and allegiance were due....
But in all this He would not seek power or exaltation for Himself contrary to God's plan, but would
exalt the Father's glory, and execute His purposes
of beneficence and love. (Ibid., p. 36).

What an example for all the hosts of heaven, and for all created beings inhabiting the myriads of worlds throughout the universe! The beloved Prince of heaven, equal with His Father in
majesty and power, yet dedicating Himself to one purpose—that
of displaying the glory and character of His Father to all creation.

Chapter 2

Lucifer's Rebellion

The stage was now set for decisions to be made among the hosts of heaven. Lucifer had made his challenge to the heavenly trio who comprised the divine Godhead. He reasoned with himself and others that his own position was inadequate for the magnitude of his gifts and intellectual abilities, and that on this basis, he should be promoted to a place in the Godhead equal to, or even above, the Son of God. In answer to this challenge, the Father Himself had set forth the eternal equality of His Son as co-regent, companion, and Creator of all worlds, including the angels themselves. Everything and everyone in the universe came from the Father through His beloved Son, and no one ever could or ever would be allowed to assume the same authority and power and as the three divine personages—Father, Son, and Holy Spirit.

By such a bold and public exposition of the eternal truths concerning the differences between the Creator and those whom He had created, the King of the universe had opened the mysteries of the Godhead as much as possible for all to consider, and weigh the consequences of rebelling against the realities which were made so clear to all the intelligent beings in heaven and upon the other worlds. Almost breathlessly, they waited for a decision from Lucifer. Would he gratefully accept the divine explanation and cheerfully resume his ordained position beside the throne—or—tragically challenge His Creator and take his stand against the truths so graciously given to help him avert the doom that surely awaited him and his followers.

For a time, Lucifer's heart was torn between submission and rebellion. At times he felt a wave of love flow over him as he recalled the many happy hours spent communing with Father and Son; the glories of working for and with his beloved Commander and representing Him to the angels who were subject to his leadership. What could possibly compare with the beauty of God's garden home, centered in the heavenly city, with the majesty of His throne flashing brilliant colors out into the universe and beyond? What thrill could be greater than leading the heavenly choir, and hearing the transcendent music which he himself had composed for the praise and honor of his Creator? To leave all this seemed at first unthinkable! What fate awaited him? Would his attempt to lead his faithful sympathizers to attack the throne be successful—or would they seal themselves forever outside of the gates of the only home they had ever known?

Questions, emotions, fears, and hope for the triumph of his cause swirled in his head, almost suffocating him. At last a steely determination grew in him, beginning small at first, but developing quickly into a rebellious rage. How could he allow himself to be so weak and vacillating? What would his followers think if they knew of his questions and fears? Already he could sense a spirit of questioning and uneasiness stirring among those who were trusting in him to decide. He must arise and act before the momentum of his cause dwindled, allowing the possibility of defection from his ranks. As their leader he must not show weakness and indecision. To inspire the courage of others, he must act at once. His decision was made. He would storm the throne of the universe! He would not lose, because his cause was just! He was the rightful sovereign who should sit upon the throne!

With a cry, he summoned his followers. Shouting and scream-
ing threats and imprecations, the myriads of now-fallen angels
comprising his army flowed like a river toward the throne of the
King and His Son. Suddenly a blinding glory flashed from their
presence. Back, back the rebellious hosts fell to escape from the
consuming fire. Before it had hardly begun, the war was over.
Down they fell into the black abyss and swirling madness they had
created, until they reached the confinement of their new abode—
an unoccupied planet called Earth. Water and darkness surrounded the planet. There was no place to set their feet, to rest and
think, to enjoy beauty, or to contemplate their fate. They were
alone in an uninhabitable place in the universe, far—so very far—
from their beautiful heavenly home.

Stunned and silent they looked about them. What would life
hold for them now? Lucifer had withdrawn himself from their
presence to a location unknown to them. Confusion reigned for
a time as they began to quarrel and blame one another for suc-
cumbing to such a foolish venture. How could they think of con-
quering the power and glory of the Eternal One? How could they
have been deceived into following Lucifer and agreeing with his
exaggerated pride? It all seemed so clear now. They had been
wrong! Both God and His Son had instructed and warned them
very clearly, but they were too entranced with Lucifer's promises
of personal advancement and position to detect the error of his
thinking that seemed so clear to them now.

Presently Lucifer returned. He had been thinking about a
plan, he said. He too could see the error of his ways. He knew the
loving character of God. Surely if they could get an audience with
the Son and convince Him of their sincere repentance and their
willingness and desire to return to their positions—or even lower
ones where they could continue to live and serve their Creator,
they could be received back into divine favor. He, Lucifer, would
solicit one of the passing loyal angels to arrange a meeting with

God's Son, and petition Him to ask for an audience with the Father. Surely in His love He would extend the scepter to them and allow them to return.

The plan seemed good to the fallen ones. What did they have to lose? Surely the love of God would prevail, and they would soon be reinstated back into heaven. Expectantly they waited for Lucifer to return from his attempted encounter with his former Commander-in Chief. When Lucifer did return, he was in a dark, angry mood. His followers were afraid to approach him. Again, he absented himself from their presence for a time. When he returned, his words were explosive and bitter. Hate poured from his heart as he hissed out the story. His appeal had been rejected! It was forever too late! There was no way back into divine favor. They had gone too far in their rebellion (White, *Early Writings*, p. 146).

But, Lucifer said, there was still a plan, an alternate one, to be sure, but a workable plan that he had conceived. Before his complete defection, he had become aware that the three members of the Godhead were making plans for the creation of a new world. In fact, this was one of the issues that goaded his jealousy, for he was not included in the planning of this new world. What if—just what if—the planet to which they had been assigned was that new world! If so, they would plan and execute a takeover. Thus they would have a place of their own to set up their kingdom and show the superiority of their government over the government of God. Eventually that would lure other worlds into joining them, and Lucifer would at last be the king of the universe, with his loyal subjects assisting him. All was not lost! They would still prevail against the now-hated God whom they once had loved and served.

Their joy and excitement knew no bounds! Lucifer had once again succeeded in his leadership and authority over them. Hilarity and pandemonium reigned for a time, and Lucifer permitted it, watching them with a sly smile. Little did they know how difficult the days ahead would be, he thought. But in his own heart he knew that the battle with heaven was not over, and that the King and His Son would not give up without a mighty struggle. He secretly wondered what God would do to thwart his evil plan.

Chapter 3

The Sacrifice

The sorrow in heaven over the fall of Lucifer and his followers can never be comprehended by mortal minds. The eternal loss of one-third of the heavenly host caused grief that only those who experienced it can know. But perhaps we can catch just a glimpse of the deep anguish of God from the following texts in Ezekiel 28:11–19.

> The word of the LORD came to me: 'Son of man, take up a lament concerning the king of Tyre and say to him: "This is what the Sovereign LORD says: 'You were the model of perfection, full of wisdom and perfect in beauty. You were in Eden, the garden of God; every precious stone adorned you … Your settings and mountings were made of gold; on the day you were created they were prepared. You were anointed as a guardian cherub, for so I ordained you. You were on the holy mount of God; you walked among the fiery stones. You were blameless in your ways from the day you were created till wickedness was found in you… You were filled with violence, and you sinned.
>
> So I drove you in disgrace from the mount of God, and I expelled you, guardian cherub, from among the fiery stones. Your heart became proud

on account of your beauty, and you corrupted your wisdom because of your splendor. So I threw you to the earth; I made a spectacle of you before kings. By your many sins and dishonest trade you have desecrated your sanctuaries. So I made a fire come out from you, and it consumed you, and I reduced you to ashes on the ground in the sight of all who were watching. All the nations who knew you are appalled at you; you have come to a horrible end and will be no more.

Ezekiel was told that this passage was to be called a "lament." Since this is a word that is infrequently used in modern society, I will refer to the Webster's dictionary, and also the New International Version (NIV) and King James Version (KJV) concordances for a better understanding.

- Webster's Dictionary: to mourn for, or show or feel regret for; an expression of mourning or grieving.
- NIV and KJV concordances: lament, mourning song, dirge; weeping, wailing (as accompanied by beating the breasts or on instruments).

From these emotional words we can see that God Himself was deeply pained by the direction Lucifer had taken. Looking into the future He saw the eventual destruction of Lucifer and his followers, and He mourned for the terrible eternal loss of this special son who was once a friend and coworker of the highest order possible among the heavenly hosts. Everything had been done to prevent his defection, but to no avail. Pride triumphed over love, respect, and reverence, and the fateful decision was made against all the evidence given and efforts made by God and the loyal angels.

Satan, the chief of the fallen angels, once had an exalted position in heaven. He was next in honor to Christ. The knowledge which he, as well as the angels who fell with him had of the character of God, of His goodness, His mercy, wisdom, and excellent glory, made their guilt unpardonable ... There were no new and wonderful exhibitions of God's exalted power that could impress them so deeply as they already experienced ... They could not be placed in a more favorable position to be proved. There was no reserve force of power, nor were there any greater heights and depths of infinite glory to overpower their jealous doubts and rebellious murmuring. (White, "Redemption—No. 1," *The Review and Herald,* February 24, 1874)

Instead of seeking to make God supreme in the affections and allegiance of his creatures, it was Lucifer's endeavor to win their service and homage to himself. And, coveting the honor which the infinite Father had bestowed upon his Son, the prince of angels aspired to power which it was the prerogative of Christ alone to wield. (White, *The Great Controversy*, p. 494).

To the very close of the controversy in Heaven, the great usurper continued to justify himself.... With one accord, Satan and his hosts threw the blame of their rebellion wholly upon Christ, declaring that if they had not been reproved, they would not have rebelled. (Ibid., pp. 499, 500)

"Satan fell from his high position through self-exaltation ... He fell for the same reason that thousands are falling today, because of an ambition to be first, an unwillingness to be under restraint" (White, Manuscript Releases, vol. 11, p. 367).

Another passage of Scripture which reveals God's reaction to even earthly rulers who, like Lucifer, use their God-given authority to arrogantly assert themselves over God's plan for them is recorded in Ezekiel 31:2–14.

> Son of man, say to Pharaoh, king of Egypt and to his hoards: 'Who can be compared with you in majesty? Consider Assyria, once a cedar in Lebanon, with beautiful branches overshadowing the forest; it towered on high, its top above the thick foliage. The waters nourished it, deep springs made it grow tall … So it towered higher than all the trees of the field … for its roots went down to abundant waters. The cedars in the garden of God could not rival it … I made it beautiful with abundant branches, the envy of all the trees of Eden in the garden of God.
>
> Therefore this is what the Sovereign LORD says: Because it towered on high, lifting its top above the think foliage, and because it was proud of its height, I handed it over to the ruler of nations, for him to deal with according to its wickedness … Therefore no other trees by the waters are ever to tower proudly on high, lifting their tops above the thick foliage. No other trees so well-watered are ever to reach such a height; they are all destined for death, for the earth below, among mortal men, with those who go down to the pit.

Notice the principle set forth here that when God's created beings fail and are lost, their exact blueprint is never repeated.

There will never be another Lucifer. We know that the mighty angel, Gabriel, took his place as the companion of Christ and the angelic representative of the Godhead, but his character is vastly different. In spite of the glory and power given him, his humility is like that of Christ. This is revealed in the conversation recorded in Revelation 19:10: "At this I fell at his feet to worship him. But he said to me, 'Do not do it! I am a fellow servant with you and with your brothers who hold to [or have, KJV] the testimony of Jesus. Worship God!'"

What a beautiful spirit! And how unlike Lucifer, who once held the same position in the heavenly courts!

So we see that in spite of the severity of the loss of Lucifer and his followers to heaven's society, God was ready to meet the challenge. Nothing is ever really lost in God's economy. Even nature is created to absorb and redistribute the elements of Earth and the firmament surrounding us. So others would take the places of those who fell. As is pointed out in the parable of the talents in Matthew 25:14–30, the talent of the unfaithful servant was removed and given to the servant who had ten talents, and the servant himself was cast out of the presence of his master into outer darkness, or oblivion.

Another example of this principle is found in Isaiah 65:11–17:

> "'But as for you who forsake the LORD and forget my holy mountain ... I will destine you for the sword ... for I called but you did not answer, I spoke but you did not listen. You did evil in my sight and chose what displeases me.' Therefore this is what the Sovereign LORD says: 'My servants will eat, but you will go hungry; my servants will drink, but you will go thirsty; my servants will rejoice, but you will be put to shame ... You will leave your name [character/blueprint] to my chosen ones as

a curse; the Sovereign LORD will put you to death,
but to His servants He will give another name...
For the past troubles will be forgotten and hidden
from my eyes. Behold, I will create new heavens
and a new earth. The former things will not be remembered, nor will they come to mind."

Eventually even the evil spirits will be destroyed and forgotten, as described in the following verses.

"O LORD, our God, other lords besides you have ruled over us,
but your name alone do we honor. They are now dead, they live
no more; those departed spirits do not rise. You punished them
and brought them to ruin; you wiped out all memory of them"
(Isa. 26:13, 14).

So although God and all of heaven mourned for the loss of
the rebellious angels, when the time of their mourning had ended,
the members of the Godhead turned their attention to the plan
that had been formulated during the eons of time for just such an
emergency. God was now ready to set in motion the divine actions
that would finally put an end to evil forever, and restore peace and
harmony to the universe.

God had a knowledge of the events of the future,
even before the creation of this world. He did
not make his purposes to fit circumstances, but
he allowed matters to develop and work out. He
did not work to bring about a certain condition of
things, but he knew that such a condition would
exist. The plan that should be carried out upon
the defection of any of the high intelligences of
heaven,—this is the secret, the mystery which
has been hid from ages. And an offering was prepared in the eternal purposes to do the very work

> which God has done for fallen humanity. (White,
> "The Mystery of God," *The Signs of the Times*,
> March 25, 1897)

Thus the very Being whose position in the Godhead had pre-
cipitated the envy and jealousy of Lucifer—the Beloved of the
Father and the joy of His heart of love—was destined to become
the only One in all of heaven and earth who could stop the dreadful curse of sin from spreading to the universe. It was He who
would step down from majesty to a manger, from glory to a cross.
It was He who must dispel forever the questions raised by Lucifer
about the character of the Father. He must display a love so powerful, so selfless, so winsome and compelling that none could ever
doubt its nature again. And He must do it on the very ground
which Lucifer would claim as his own. The risk was staggering; to
lose would be unthinkable.

And now the divine trio went into seclusion. Who can know
what feelings of grief and sorrow they endured at the prospect before them? The thought of separation must have seemed unbear-
able for a time. But there was no other way—the eternal plan must
be carried out, whatever the risk and sacrifice it would mean to the
Father and the Son. They knew that love must triumph over the
false accusations of the evil one. The price to be paid was great,
but the results of the sacrifice made would forever inoculate the
kingdom of God from further rebellion.

Together they came forth to announce the plan to the waiting
heavenly hosts.

Chapter 4

The Plan

With great reverence the angelic host approached the throne and waited for the Father and Son to speak. The Father spoke first. A plan had been formulated, He said, which would eventually restore all that had been lost by Lucifer's defection. The first step would be the restoration of the places vacated by the fallen angels. But no one would be allowed to assume these positions until they had been tested and proven to be eternally reliable, never again to repeat the tragedy that the experiment into sin had caused. Since all the loyal angels had already been proven, those who would take the places of the fallen angels must also have an opportunity to be tested and to show that they understood and agreed with the eternal principles of God's government.

The loyal angels listened with rapt attention. What could be the answer to the dilemma? How could newly-created beings be tested to the same level that they themselves had been tested as the deceptions of Lucifer developed right in their midst? It had been so difficult to perceive the motives of the father of lies as he shared with them his specious reasoning and accusations concerning the character of God. Eventually it became clear to them that their beloved angelic leader had become an enemy—something completely unknown in the society of heaven until that point. With intense interest they continued listening as the Son of God began to speak.

"My Father and I have a joyous announcement to make to all of you," He said. "We have grieved over the tremendous pressure placed upon you to withstand the temptations of the disloyal angels. You have valiantly stood for my Father and me and the principles of our government. You have proved that you can be trusted to be placed in any position and be true to the throne. That will be eminently important in the days ahead, as we progress into the next phase of the war for righteousness. The battle is not over—it has just begun."

"As you know," continued the Father, "Lucifer and his followers have been assigned to the planet called earth. He will be granted a time of probation during which he will be allowed to demonstrate the outworking of the principles of his government. From now on, he is to be called, 'Satan,' which means 'adversary, accuser, slanderer,' for he is no longer a light-bearer from the throne of heaven, but now is a hostile enemy of all goodness and righteousness. When his probation is ended, he and his followers will be eternally destroyed."

Again the Son began to speak. "In spite of the immense suffering that Satan's sin has caused all of us, the Father and I will go forward with our plans to create a beautiful new world on planet earth. We will fill it with verdant vegetation, animals and birds of all kinds, and crown it with a new order of beings called 'man.' They will be created in our image in a very unique and special way, so that we can demonstrate the relationship of love that exists in the Godhead. While in heaven, Lucifer charged us with the accusation of unfair exclusiveness. By creating these beautiful beings in our image and likeness, we will show the way our love works for the good of all who are a part of our great family. The love that we have for each other is the love that we give to each of you, and then extends to envelop and enrich all who live by the power of our love. Please rejoice with us as we plan this new world—the place where our love will be demonstrated in the most dramatic way possible for the entire universe to observe and understand, and to answer all questions about us once and for all time!"

The angels were enraptured by the majesty of the plan presented to them, and with one accord began to fill the courts of heaven with sublime songs of praise to their Creator. "Holy, holy, holy, Lord God Almighty, who was and is and is to come! May He reign forever in majesty and purity; may His love and surpassing glory fill the heavens and the earth!"

When the songs had died away, God the Father spoke again: "Thank you all for your support and the outpouring of your love! Your cooperation and assistance will be vital to the success of the conquest and victory over the forces of evil in the days ahead. But there is another part of the plan that must now be revealed to you. I will ask my Son to tell you what must happen before the war with Satan is over.

For a moment the Son stood silently before them in His most majestic appearance. His face beamed with the light and glory of His Father, and radiated with such unutterable love and *pathos* that some of the angels veiled their faces, and others gazed at Him, entranced by the emotions that were coming from Him, sensing that He was wrestling with something of so great importance that He was at once loath and yet longing to tell them. And then He began to speak.

"From eternity my Father and I have had a solemn covenant that should any of our created beings defect and rebel against the principles of our government, there would need to be a divine emissary, a representative to go to the place where love ceased to rule in the hearts of the people, and a kingdom based on selfishness would spring up and begin to spread its venom to others. Until now, all created worlds have enjoyed the freedom of choice which we give to everyone, yet not one has chosen to manifest doubt and defiance against the law of love and liberty by which my Father and I govern the universe.

"But a dangerous situation has now arisen which knows no precedent. Therefore, we have chosen earth to be the place where the greatest demonstration of our love and government will be displayed. Two beautiful, perfect people will be placed there in a garden home which will be a replica of the garden that contains our throne. They will have a tree of life and a river of life from which they can partake and live forever. It will be a special place where we can meet personally with them and instruct them.

"But because they too will have freedom of choice, and since they must be tested on every point as each of you have been, another tree, called the tree of knowledge of good and evil, will also be planted in the center of the garden. Satan will be allowed access only to this tree. They will be instructed not to eat of this tree, for in so doing, they would prove themselves to be disloyal, and death would be the result, just as surely as it is the fate of all who rebel against the government of God. They also will be instructed to always remain together to help each other stay away from the tree lest they be ensnared by Satan's wily temptations. If they stand the test and be obedient to these instructions, after a period of time they will be accounted worthy to join the ranks of heaven and fill the positions that once were held by Lucifer and his followers.

"However, if man should fall prey to the evil one and succumb to his lies, another plan must immediately take effect to rescue them from the results of their disobedience. From eternity the Father and I have covenanted together that if such a problem should ever arise, I, as the Son, would go to the fallen race as the representative of the Father, live among them as one of them, and by my life give a visible example of the loving obedience to the Father's principles which are required to live in His presence. Because I would be living in the kingdom of the evil one, his hatred for me will result in my death. But by that death, the self-sacrificing love of the Father's heart will be fully displayed, and any doubt of His goodness dispelled forever. From that death I will rise again to life and come back to join you as we work together to minister to all who will accept the principles of the kingdom of heaven, and receive my life into their minds and hearts. Eventually when the members of my kingdom are complete, I will return to earth and receive the full number of those who will choose to be saved by my sacrifice, and bring them back to join us in heaven forever."

With cries of anguish, the angelic host moved forward toward the throne, and as one man, threw themselves at the feet of their beloved Commander. All expressed their willingness and desire to take the place of the Son of God on this mission to earth that would result in His suffering and death. Lovingly, and with His tears mingling with theirs, He lifted them up and assured them that although they could not take His place, for only one equal with the Father could pay the price for sin, they would be of inestimable worth to Him, attending Him every moment, giving Him comfort and courage, bringing light from heaven, helping Him to reach hearts, protecting His followers, and pushing back the hosts of the enemy. They would be His companions and helpers, making His mission possible, and finally, guarding His grave, then calling Him forth on resurrection morning and joining Him on His triumphal entry through the pearly gates back into the Father's arms.

On hearing this, tears of sorrow turned to tears of joy! Someday the journey would be over, the plan of salvation complete, the war would be won, and the victorious sons of God would join them in eternal triumph over the evil one! With anticipation for that glorious day, they could now turn their attention to the next phase of the plan of rescue, as the three members of the Godhead prepared for the creation of the beautiful new world.

> God created man for His glory. It was His purpose to repopulate heaven with the human race, when, after a period of test and trial, they had proved to be loyal to Him. Adam was to be tested to see whether he would be obedient. Had he stood the test, his thoughts would have been as the thoughts

of God, his character would have been molded af-
ter the similitude of the divine character. (White,
"God's Purpose for Us," *The Signs of the Times*,
May 29, 1901)

"Jesus came to our world to dispute the authority of Satan. He
came to restore in man the defaced image of God, to raise him, to
elevate him, fit him for companionship with the angels of heaven,
to take the position in the courts of God which Satan forfeited
through rebellion" (White, "The Liquor Traffic Working Counter
to Christ," *The Review and Herald*, May 8, 1894).

"The vacancies made in heaven by the fall of Satan and his angels will be filled by the redeemed of the Lord" (White, "Christ's
Ambassadors," *The Review and Herald,* May 29, 1900)

Chapter 5

The Creation

The angels never tire of watching the members of the Godhead as they create new worlds. No two are exactly alike, and yet there is a purpose for each; for everything God creates, from the smallest atom to the largest sphere in the universe, reflects something about His character of love. The galaxies that circle endlessly about His throne speak of His majesty and power. The snowflake reflects His beauty and purity and perfect attention to every detail. From the birds that fly around the world to the smallest insect that creeps upon the earth, God reveals an aspect of Himself.

But nowhere in the universe has there ever been a world so important as the creation upon planet Earth. Light, air, vegetation, sun, moon and stars; water, sky, and earth teeming with living creatures—the activities of each day progressed toward the supreme act of the creation of a new order of beings, called, "man" (*Sons and Daughters of God*, p. 7). And when everything was in place to provide for his happiness, God created Adam. Stooping down to gather some clay, He fashioned a body so majestic, so noble that all could see that it was designed after the pattern of Himself. He then breathed into that clay form the breath of His own nostrils, and instantly life flowed into every sinew and cell of Adam's body, and his eyes opened to see the beautiful smile of his Creator, inviting him to rise and walk with Him on a tour of his garden home.

Beautiful, loving animals of all description came parading by, birds flitted near, flowers nodded to the new prince. All of nature seemed subject to him as Adam surveyed his kingdom for the first time. Delighted, he gave names to each living creature, sensing the uniqueness of each blueprint. Patiently God waited for something to stir in Adam's breast. There were two of each kind, gamboling about, playing together, joyous in the rich bounty of their new home. Noticing this, Adam wondered if there was someone, somewhere, like himself. Was he also to have a mate? Smiling, God bade him rest on a grassy bed, and as he slept, a miracle was born.

Taking a rib from Adam's side, God formed a suitable companion for him, and brought her to his side. She, too, was created in God's image and filled by His Holy Spirit. Like Adam, Eve was clothed with a glow of light reflecting the outshining of God's own glory, which represented their perfect harmony with His character in mind, body and soul.

Adam awakened and sat up, rubbing the sleep from his eyes, wondering why God had felt he needed to rest when he had felt no weariness. Suddenly he felt a gentle touch on his arm, and a soft, musical voice spoke his name. "Adam!"

He turned quickly to see who had spoken to him, and there, sitting beside him was the most beautiful creature he had ever seen. She looked somewhat like himself, he thought, but ever so much more beautiful! Her long, flowing hair caressed her shoulders, and her face—oh, her face! Delicate, perfect features, intelligent, loving eyes, transparent blue like the pools in the garden—how they captured him in their gaze!

"Adam," she spoke again, "I have been created by God to be your companion! He saw your loneliness, and while you slept He took a rib from your side, and from that rib He created me! I am a part of you, Adam, and I am here to be your helper in everything you do. He has placed a great love for you in my heart, and I want so much to bring happiness and joy to you! We will always be together, for God has instructed me to always stay by your side.

Together we are to have dominion over the earth and its crea-tures—you as the head of the nations that will come from us, and I as the recipient of your love and protection, and your support in every aspect of life. Are you pleased with me, Adam? Will you ac-cept me as God's special gift to you?"

For a moment no words could escape from Adam's lips. Pleased? His heart seemed ready to burst with emotion and love for God and for his beautiful companion. His heart sang and leaped, trying to find words to express his joy.

"Pleased?" he said. "I am more than pleased! I am filled with praise to God, and love for you, my beloved. You are more than I could have imagined—you are the answer to my heart's desire, my longing, and my loneliness. You are bone of my bones and flesh of my flesh—my second self! (*Patriarchs and Prophets*, p. 46). I am determined that we shall never be separated, always working together, rejoicing together, worshipping our Creator together. My happiness knows no bounds! You are my 'Eve,' my life (*NIV Concordance*), and the mother of all life that comes from our union. May God bless our home which He has established, and our union which He has ordained."

Suddenly the pair became aware of the presence of their Creator, who had been watching them with pleasure. He came forward and embraced them both, and blessed them. "Be fruitful and multiply," He said. "May your descendants be like the sands of the sea and the stars of the sky. May those who come from you be children of light, and loyal subjects of God's kingdom of righ-teousness. I bequeath to you this earth and all that is in it, which has been created for your happiness. You may eat of every good thing that I have placed here for you. Only one thing is denied to you—you must not go near the tree of knowledge of good and evil or eat of its fruit. To do so would result in death, for it is the one place in your entire world where the enemy, Satan, is allowed to come. He is a defector from the courts of heaven, and the father of all lies. His power to deceive is great; therefore you must not go near the tree to watch or listen to him speak to you. Angels of light will instruct you further about the great war that he started in heaven before the world was created.

"But come! Let us go to the tree of life that I have planted in the center of the garden for you. Here! Pluck and eat freely of its fruit, for to eat of it gives the freshness and vigor of eternal life! It is My gift to you, and as long as you are obedient and faithful to My instructions, you may eat of it and live forever, just as do the angels around My throne!

"Now, My children, I have one more precious gift to give to you. Sit down with Me on the grass beside the river of life. I have something to tell you about the special Day of Rest that I am about to inaugurate for your enjoyment and spiritual completion. It will be a weekly twenty-four hour period of time when I will meet with you in special communion. As you see, the sun is beginning to hover over the horizon. Twilight will soon begin. Every seventh day, this will be the sign that I am coming to spend that day with you. I will look forward with anticipation to those hours to visit together with you, after your busy week. Angels will always accompany Me, and make our time together even more joyous! I have called for some to join us, and they are arriving just now! Come, My beloved children! Let us begin the sacred celebration of our first Sabbath together!

Chapter 6

The Fall

It was heaven on earth for a time. Everything functioned just the way it was meant to be. Then one day Eve innocently slipped away from Adam's side. She hardly noticed the passing moments as she tended the special garden of roses she had planted along the pathway to the tree of life. How beautiful they were that morning in their varied colors and fragrances. They lifted their faces to greet her as she stooped to touch the delicate petals of each flower. Her heart sang with joy and praise to the Creator, whose presence seemed especially near that morning, as if He were there with her to savor and approve of her pleasant labors for Him and for her husband.

Ah, yes! Where was Adam? Her glance caught his form some distance away, where he was busily training the bowers around the area they had chosen for rest after the labors of the day. He had not noticed her absence, she presumed. For a moment she hesitated. Just then a bird flashed by with brightly colored plumage, and settled on a branch just above her. It was one that she had often seen while working in her rose garden. She watched his tiny throat swell and pulsate as he sang for her in lovely trills and melodies. "Come, lovely one! Sit on my finger for a moment!" The tiny bird hovered just out of her reach, and then flew to a branch a little farther down the path. Eve looked toward the center of the garden, and gazed for a moment at the tree of knowledge. She noticed that it seemed to be glowing more brightly than usual, its lovely fruit glistening like balls of fire in the morning sun.

A sudden chill flashed through her body as she recalled the warning given by God; but she reassured herself that she was strong and wise enough to perceive and resist all evil (White, *Patriarchs and Prophets*, p. 54). Venturing closer, she saw a beautiful serpent winging its way into the branches of the tree. With a brilliant covering resembling burnished gold (White, *Selected Messages,* book 3, p. 40), it shimmered in the sunlight with flashing rainbow colors. Eve had often wondered about this unique animal. He seemed to have such wisdom in his eyes. Sometimes she wondered what thoughts he might reveal if he could converse in human language.

As Eve continued to watch, the serpent began to eat the fruit of the forbidden tree! Amazed, she wondered—would the serpent die as God had told them would be their fate if they should eat the fruit of this tree? She ventured closer. Questions swirled in her mind. Why was the serpent permitted to go freely to the forbidden tree and eat of its fruit, while she and Adam were restricted from either eating or touching it?

As if in answer to her thoughts, she heard a melodious voice coming from the tree. "Eve!" Shocked and frightened, she looked for the origin of the voice.

"Don't be afraid, Eve. It is just I, the serpent that you have been watching. I have come here to partake of some of the fruit of this tree. It has magical powers beyond any of the other trees. Has God told you that you are not to eat of the fruit of this tree?"

"Yes," she replied. "He has warned us not to eat of it or touch it lest we die!"

"Of course," he replied with a slight sneer in his voice. "God knows that if you do, you will be like gods, knowing both good and evil. You will *not* surely die! Behold what the tree has done for me! Have you ever seen any of the other creatures of the garden talking to you as I am? It is because I eat regularly the fruit of this tree, and its magical powers are transmitted into my brain so that I can think and speak like you!

"Just imagine, Eve, what this fruit would do for you! If I, a lower creature, have been elevated to be able to converse with you, surely you, a higher being, would be elevated to the level of God Himself! The tree of life energizes your body and gives you eternal life. But *this* tree energizes your mind and gives you the powers of unlimited mental development that God has! Here, Eve, eat and experience the transformation that will give you every desire of your heart!"

Eve looked at the fruit that the serpent had placed in her hands. The reasoning of his words seemed flawless and convincing. Why would God create something so important as this fruit, and then restrict them from partaking of it? Quickly she put it to her mouth. Tasting its delicious flavor, she ate with heightening anticipation of the outcome the serpent had promised.

Soon she became aware of a thrill flowing through her whole body. Quickly plucking several pieces of fruit from the low hanging branches, she ran to share her amazing discovery with her husband.

Adam looked up from his task. Eve was swiftly approaching, her face flushed with an unusual excitement.

"Adam," she cried out as she came toward him. "Adam, I just met the most unusual creature I have yet seen in our garden. Surely you remember the beautiful winged serpent that we have at times seen flying from tree to tree. Really, Adam, I didn't intend to wander so far. I was tending to my rose garden down the path to the tree of life. But as I was about to come back to your side, I caught sight of the forbidden tree. Oh Adam, how brilliantly it shone in the morning sun! As I was wondering why it seemed unusually bright, I saw the serpent flying to the branches of the tree. He looked so beautiful so I went a little closer to observe him.

"And then the most astounding thing happened, Adam! He began to pluck and eat the fruit of the tree! I wondered if he might die, but he didn't! And then he began talking to me in our language, just like one of us! He told me that the tree has magical powers to make us so wise that we would be as gods, knowing both good and evil. I ate some of the fruit myself, and I feel such exhilaration that I have never before experienced! I have brought some of the fruit for you, my love, and we can eat it together. Can you not see what it has done for me, Adam? Please taste it, and you will see for yourself what it will do to enhance the powers of your mind!"

Smiling sweetly, Eve reached out toward him with a choice piece of fruit in her hand. "Adam, please just taste it and you will see what I mean! The fruit is not poisonous at all! I am proof that no harm will come to you if you will eat of it as I have. In fact, you will be greatly blessed by its power to enlighten your mind and energize your body. I have never felt so alive as I do now!"

Adam knew instantly what had happened. The enemy God had warned them about had somehow used the serpent to lure her to the tree, and then succeeded in convincing her to eat of the forbidden fruit. And now she stood before him, looking even more beautiful and beguiling than he could remember. The thought of being separated from her tore through his heart. How could he have been so careless as to permit her to be absent from his side for so long? It was clearly his fault, he thought, and now he must pay the price for his negligence. He must partake of the fruit with her and share her fate. Surely God would provide a way for them to stay together and be received back into His favor. Perhaps she was even right, for he could see no difference in her that would warn of impending doom. Yes, he would join her—the decision was made. He quickly took the apple from her hand and bit into the sweet, juicy fruit.

Chapter 7

The Covering

At first Adam, too, felt a sense of exhilaration. Everything seemed brighter, his mind clearer, and the feelings in his body more intense. But soon a foreboding came over him, and a sense of approaching doom settled upon him. Suddenly he noticed that the beautiful robe of light that had always clothed them had disappeared, and they were naked! A chill shook his body. What could this mean? Surely it must portend evil for them both. Taking Eve's hand, he ran toward a row of trees near the edge of the garden. Breathing heavily, he clutched at the branches, stripping as many leaves as he could, and began tying the stems together. Eve understood what Adam was trying to do, and she joined him in finishing the task of forming flimsy garments to cover their nakedness.

Hardly had they finished, when they heard a familiar voice from the other side of the garden. Of course! It was the time of day when God came to visit and talk with them! Instinctively and in terror, they hid themselves behind the trees, hoping that their garments of leaves would help them blend with the foliage and thus be invisible to the searching eye of their Creator.

"Adam! Where are you?" The call was loving, gentle, but insistent.

Adam tried to resist, to continue hiding, but he could not. Something in that loving voice compelled him to obey. Taking Eve's hand, he stepped out through an opening in the trees into the soft glow of the evening sky, and came face to face with His Lord.

"My children, what have you done? Adam, have you eaten fruit from the tree which I commanded you not to eat?"

"Yes, Lord, I did eat of it, but it was Eve—the wife You gave me—who tempted me to eat. She brought fruit for me from the tree and urged me, saying that she had already eaten from it and did not die. She then offered it to me, and seeing that she seemed to have no ill effects from eating it, I also took the fruit and ate some of it."

"Eve, did you do this thing which I warned you not to do, and did you also beguile your husband to join you in eating the fruit of the forbidden tree?"

"Yes, my Lord, I did eat some of the fruit from the tree," Eve replied. "But the serpent was so wise and beautiful, and he told me I would not die, but become as wise as You! I thought how desirable that would be, and so I ate, and also brought some of the fruit to my husband so that we could eat it together."

"Because you have done this thing which I commanded you not to do, I must now, in sorrow, tell you what the results of your choice will be. Before the sun goes down, you must leave your beautiful home and live outside the garden. You may never step inside its gates again, for your hearts have become changed toward Me, and your ability to obey my laws has become damaged. To eat of the tree of life would perpetuate your fallen nature forever, and I cannot allow this to happen. My love for you is still the same, but the rules that govern our relationship must change. I can no longer visit with you and speak to you freely face to face, for My glory would consume you.

"My kingdom is based upon the harmony and agreement of My subjects with My character and My law of love. All are given the freedom to choose. Lucifer was the first to challenge the principles by which I govern the universe, and he was given ample time to consider carefully the pathway of rebellion. When he made his final choice and tried to usurp the throne of heaven, he had to be expelled, and his sympathizers with him. As you know, they have been expelled to this earth. You have been created to head a race of beings upon earth who will recognize the fallacies of Satan's accusations against My character, My law, and the principles of My government, and if faithful, to take the places of the angels who fell.

"It was My fervent desire that you would follow my instructions carefully, and choose not to tamper with the delusions of the enemy. But now that you, Adam, have listened to the voice of your wife instead of my instructions, and you, Eve, have listened to the deceptions of the enemy and tempted your husband to disobey me, I must initiate an alternate plan to intervene for you, or death will surely be your fate.

"Adam, please go to the area of the garden where the sheep are getting ready to bed down for the night, and bring the choicest one to Me. And now, Eve, while he is gone, I must sadly tell you that your former state of equality with Adam must be reduced to allow for him to fully develop his leadership as the rightful prince of this earth. It was my intention to allow you to gradually observe the differences between Adam's role as leader, and your role as his helper—equal to him, yet submissive to him in the same way that I, the Son of God, am equal to My Father, and yet I am also submissive to Him. It is a great mystery—one that Lucifer never understood in heaven—but one that is vital to the power of the love that flows between Us, and from Us flows out to all created beings.

"But because you have assumed the position of leadership over your husband, and that he has submitted to your pleadings and disobeyed my commands, you must now learn under more difficult circumstances than you can now imagine, to be in submission to Adam as the head of the family that you will produce after leaving this garden home. What you could have learned in a perfect environment, you will now learn in a much more difficult setting. But always remember that I will be with you by My Spirit, and you will have the help of angels from heaven to give you the grace to overcome, and to be the beautiful daughter I created you to be. You will be the center of the radiance of My love in your home, and your husband and children will rise up and call you blessed.

"I see that Adam is now returning, with a fine ram by his side. Adam! Please bring the ram to Me.

"Adam and Eve, I am now going to establish a ritual for you to follow for the rest of your days on earth. You cannot completely understand the meaning of this ritual right now. I am sure that you remember My warning that should you disobey my instructions, in that very day you would die. But before the creation of this world, the Father and I formulated a plan, that if you broke the covenant that We gave you, and fell into sin, a time of grace would be given you to rescue you from eternal death. But to do this, the consequences of your sin must fall on a substitute. Someday I Myself will be that substitute. At a future time, I will come to this earth, be born as a helpless baby, and live perfectly the life that you should have lived in harmony with My laws. Then I will die as the innocent substitute for you, and for all who will accept My sacrifice for their sins and come into full agreement with My law of love.

"I have chosen this patient, loving animal as an example of the character of the Father and the Son. And I, as my Father's representative to you, and to help you understand and serve us from love, must be the ultimate sacrifice which will cover your na-kedness and shield you from the assaults of the evil one, for he will now have access to you as you leave the garden. I can protect you as long as you look to Me and follow My counsel. In this way, the relationship of love and trust we have always had until today will be continued. Though you will not see Me again in person, you can see me in this ritual, and remember that I am always there for you. As you wear the garments that I am providing for you from the skins of animals such as this (Gen. 3:21), let their warmth and protection bring you comfort that I have not abandoned you, for I will never leave nor forsake you. (Heb. 13:5, 6.) You will never be alone, for I will assign My angels to bring the light of My presence to you, and to guard you in all your ways (Ps. 91:11).

"But I have one more loving reminder for you before we part. Always remember to keep the weekly appointment that we have every seventh day of the week. As the sun goes down on the evening of the sixth day, I will bring a company of angels with Me as I come to join you for the sacred celebration of the Sabbath, just as I did on our first Sabbath together. I will eagerly look forward to those precious hours, for I will miss you more than you can know.

"Now let us be going! I will walk with you to the outer gate of the garden. The garments I promised you are ready, and will be given you before you leave. They are My parting gifts to you. You will need their covering, for the sun is lowering in the evening sky."

Sorrowfully, Adam and Eve walked together with their Lord for the last time. They saw the shining cherubim waiting for them at the gate. Donning the warm coverings God had provided, they turned to hear once more the loving voice they had always eagerly anticipated each evening when He came to visit with them. But this time, the pain of what they had done was too great to enjoy the moment. As they gazed into His eyes for the last time, they saw only love and mercy. Raising His arms in His customary manner of blessing, He lingered for a moment, and then disappeared from their sight. As they turned, they gazed wonderingly at the two cherubim who were now stationed at the garden gate, with flashing swords shining in every direction to forever protect the sacred precincts from any access to the tree of life.

Hand in hand, with tears flowing down their faces, they stepped out into the growing darkness.

Chapter 8

The Sanctuary

Life was hard for Adam and Eve after they were expelled from their garden home. Thorns and thistles grew, the earth did not produce as it had before, relationships were sometimes strained, and previously unknown emotions became a part of their lot. Where there had been only joy, peace and love, they now became aware of fear, pain, anger, resentment, irritation, jealousy, grief, and all the kaleidoscope of human emotions that are common to our fallen nature. And while they did not experience fear of immediate death, they knew that the sentence had only been deferred. The sudden death of their son, Able, at the hand of his brother, brought this terrible fact into their daily lives.

Looking back upon their idyllic life in Eden, they longed for the peace and safety they had once enjoyed. While Satan was restricted to only one place in the garden, they could roam freely without danger anywhere they chose. But now, danger stalked at every turn, temptations came from within and without, and peace and safety came from only one source—the knowledge that God had promised to be with them and protect them as long as they obeyed His commands and trusted in His love for them.

As the years rolled by, they became more settled in this covenant relationship with God, and their faith in Him became unshakable. They matured in godliness, and used their influence to teach and help others to know the true character and law of God, and to follow His precepts. Some responded to their entreaties and example, and followed the simple sacrificial ceremony that Adam had learned from God that last evening in the garden. It gave them hope of better things to come—a time of restoration, and a Savior to come that by His own sacrifice would end the reign of Satan, and bring harmony once again between earth and heaven.

But the vast majority of people spurned the authority of God and did not seek to know or to follow Him. This was a continuing grief to Adam until his life came to an end, and he lay down to rest in death to await the resurrection call of his beloved Lord.

Centuries came and went with very little interference from God, for He was allowing Satan opportunity to display the outcome of the principles of his government. Using the blessing of health and vigor that was inherited from Adam, and unfettered by the ravages that sin has made upon the earth since the flood, the human race prostituted themselves to demons and debauchery. Only a few, such as Enoch and the patriarchal line coming from Adam's posterity, remained undefiled by the evil that spread across the world. Finally, Noah was chosen to preach the last warning to the people of his generation, and he and his family were the only survivors of the flood sent by God to cleanse the earth of the consequences of Satan's handiwork.

And then God went in search of a man. The time had come for God to begin the preparation for the coming of His Son. There must be a people who would understand His character and His laws, and a message that would give all people the opportunity to learn the difference between the truth of God and the lies and errors of the devil. In order to accomplish this God needed a man who would be His friend as Adam had been, who would know His voice, love and obey Him, and take His truth to the world. At the appropriate time, Abraham was chosen to be that man and to produce the nation that came through his lineage.

Again centuries passed until another man of God was called to lead the chosen nation, now a million strong, from Egypt, the land of their captivity, to Canaan, their promised inheritance. Moses, also, was a friend of God who knew Him personally on an intimate level. He could be trusted to carry out the purposes of God, to obey Him explicitly, and to be the bearer of His messages. Through him the mighty nation of Israel was delivered from the hand of Pharaoh, and God's explicit and detailed laws and regulations were given to them while they sojourned in the desert. This time, nothing was left to chance. In order to have a place prepared for His Son to be born, recognized and welcomed as the Savior and Messiah for all mankind, the people through whom He would come must be instructed and prepared to receive Him.

Until this time, the worship of God's faithful followers had continued to be based upon the slaying of a sacrificial lamb on a simple altar of stones, which was to be carried out by the father of the family or clan each morning and evening. It was the way to proclaim their faithfulness to God, and trust in a coming Redeemer. By this simple ceremony, the whole family was counted as being under the covering and protection of God, and worthy of His blessings.

But the nation of Israel was now introduced to a personal, visible God who spoke His laws to them audibly in awful majesty and grandeur, and then wrote His words upon tablets of stone. These tablets were to be preserved in an elaborate tabernacle, or sanctuary, whose services were to be detailed and specific. Priests were chosen from the tribe of Levi to serve in the sanctuary, replacing the priesthood of the father in each individual family.

Every part of this sanctuary and its services was designed to teach about God, His character, and his laws. Every detail was to explain the work of the Savior who would come, and the plan of salvation that would bring the knowledge needed by every person to see the difference between God's kingdom of love and freedom, and Satan's kingdom of deception and bondage. The sanctuary was given to bring the light and knowledge from heaven that would set people free to choose what course they would take, and to know the way back into communication and friendship with God. And it was to prepare the way for God's Son to come and display in His life the living oracles of God's law, and make it beautiful in the setting of the life He lived. In brief, these principles are summed up in Matthew 22:37–40: "'Love the Lord your God with all your heart and with all your soul and with all your mind.' This is the first and greatest commandment. And the second is like it: 'Love your neighbor as yourself.' All the Law and the Prophets hang on these two commandments."

But through the years that followed, the true meaning of the sanctuary services was lost. Rivers of blood, calloused and self-serving priests, and centuries of apathy and outright apostasy brought the people to such a low point that for four centuries after the book of Malachi was written, there were very few who heard the voice of God's Spirit, and no one through whom God could speak to communicate His will (*The SDA Bible Commentary,* vol. 4, p. 1151). Darkness covered the earth, and gross darkness enveloped the people (Isa. 60:2). The true worshippers longed for light, and for relief from the overbearing slavery of the dogmas and traditions invented by men. It was time for the Messiah to come (*The SDA Bible Commentary,* vol. 4, p. 1153).

Chapter 9

The Witness

All of heaven was astir that day. The Father and the Son had announced to the angels that it was time for the Son to leave His Father's side, and go to planet Earth on His mission to provide deliverance for every son and daughter of Adam who desired to escape from the slavery of sin, and to be restored to the innocence and purity lost in Eden.

It was a time of joy and a time of sorrow—joy for the anticipation of all the captives of Satan who would be set free, and sorrow for the unspeakable loss of the presence of their beloved Commander from the courts of heaven. He would soon become a helpless baby in the arms of His mother, Mary, the young woman chosen by the Father to bear His Child. He would be called, "Jesus," meaning, "He will save His people from their sins" (Matt. 1:21). He would become a child of earth, a Son of Adam and the long line of his inheritance that followed the Lord and practiced the principles of His kingdom. But unlike all the others, He would live the life of perfect purity that Adam lost when he fell, and through His righteous life, win back a great host of restored men and women who would connect with Him by faith.

As the time of departure grew nearer, the angels gathered around Him, and one by one, each stepped forward to embrace Him for one last time. Tears were shed, words of comfort and encouragement were spoken, and loving counsel was given for each one. At last, He stepped back, and raising His hands in blessing,

He disappeared into the secret place where He and His Father could be alone.

Who can know what happened there in those last moments of the Godhead together? Ellen White states, "The work of redemption ... is indeed the mystery by which everlasting righteousness is brought to all who believe.... Christ, at an infinite cost, by a painful process, mysterious to angels as well as to men, assumed humanity. Hiding His divinity, laying aside His glory, He was born a babe in Bethlehem" (*The SDA Bible Commentary,* vol. 7, p. 915).

Divesting Himself of the glory and visible form of His divine being, He left the presence of His Father, and came to earth. Now a tiny seed containing the full essence of His divinity and holy character, He was surrounded and protected by the Holy Spirit, and placed in the womb of a daughter of Adam, there to be joined forever to the human family.

"Therefore, when Christ came into the world, he said: 'Sacrifice and offering you did not desire, but a body you prepared for me; with burnt offerings and sin offerings you were not pleased. Then I said, 'Here I am—it is written about me in the scroll—I have come to do your will, O God'" (Heb. 10:5–7).

Psalm 40:6–8, the source quoted in Hebrews, added the words, "Your law is within my heart" (verse 8).

Now clothed with the garb of humanity, Jesus walked among men as one with us. Subject to the feelings of our infirmities, He experienced all the range of emotions that are common to mankind, yet in all of this, He did not sin (Heb. 4:15). Before His coming into the world, He and the Father carefully mapped out every aspect of His earthly life. In order to redeem man from his fallen condition, Jesus must know by experience the power of temptation in every situation. Throughout the Old Testament, Holy Spirit-inspired Messianic prophesies pointed forward to the time when He would come to tabernacle with us and show us the way back to holiness of character and life. This is why it is often mentioned in the gospels, "These things happened so that the Scripture would be fulfilled" (John 19:36).

Walking the dusty pathways of earth as a common man, Jesus encountered the problems, the joys, and the sorrows of the people with whom He lived, and His heart of love went out to each one. He had come to earth to bring the knowledge of His Father to the fallen race, and He set His course every day with this goal in mind. Constant, unbroken communion with His Father through the avenue of the Holy Spirit was absolutely essential for Him. Encumbered with the weakness of humanity, He, like us, needed to receive daily supplies of wisdom and power from the limitless resources of heaven. In His dealings with the Jewish leaders, and in contact with needy people throughout each day, He was dependent upon His Father for every word He spoke, and every deed that He performed.

"... I do nothing on my own, but speak just what the Father has taught me. The one who sent me is with me; He has not left me alone, for I always do what pleases him" (John 8:28, 29).

His nights were often spent in prayer and supplication for wisdom and strength for the coming day. While his disciples slept, He communed with His Father, receiving from Him the love and assurance that sustained Him in His daily battle with the enemy. Angels attended Him, bringing Him comfort and light from heavenly realms. In all of this, He was providing an example of the kind of relationship that anyone who desires to be an overcomer must follow.

Patiently He trod the pathway marked out for Him, never deviating from His Father's will, never breaking down under the pressure brought upon Him by men or demons. At last the time drew near for His ultimate, supreme sacrifice. He dreaded not so much the physical pain that He must endure, but the thought of being separated from the sense of His Father's presence brought agony to His soul. How could He bear the weight of the sins of the whole world without His Father's arms around Him?

As the last few days of the crucifixion week bore down upon Him, His uppermost thoughts were to prepare His disciples to face the crushing disappointment that was about to overtake them like a crouching lion about to spring. He used every moment, every opportunity to speak to them of His love; to leave an example of the lives He wanted them to live after He ascended back to His Father. He instructed them concerning the work of the Holy Spirit, who would direct the work on earth as His representative. He prayed for them (John 17) and committed them, and all those who would believe on Him through their ministry, to His Father. His work was done. Now all that remained were the "three days and three nights in the heart of the earth" (Matt. 12:40) during which He would be given over to the evil designs of the Prince of Darkness.

As Jesus and His disciples entered the Garden of Gethsemane, the disciples found a comfortable area to bed down for the night. They were accustomed to the night vigils of their Master, and though they intended to pray for a while, they were soon overcome with sleepiness. Before Jesus had slipped away to a solitary spot, He had requested that they stay awake and pray with Him. But nature took its course, and they were soon fast asleep. Meanwhile, Jesus fell to the ground in an agony that seemed to sweep over Him and clutch at His very soul. He felt the beams of the light of His Father's presence receding from Him, and a terrifying loneliness welled up as if to choke out His very life. He clutched at the ground, moaning in low, tearless sobs. "My Father! My Father! Please take this cup from me! I cannot bear to be separated from you! We have been together for eternity, one with each other, working together, sharing our love and joy with all we have created. I cannot live without you!"

The silence and darkness closed in around Him. No answer, no comforting sense of His Father's presence. He staggered to His feet, hoping to find His disciples awake and praying for Him, but alas, they were sound asleep. Aroused by His presence and the sound of His voice again imploring them to pray for Him and for themselves, they tried to obey. However, they were not able to shake off the supernatural drowsiness that Satan pressed upon them.

Again Jesus fell upon the ground, as though His life was being crushed from His body. Blood oozed from his pores and stained the ground beneath Him. In agony He cried out again, "Oh my Father, if this cup may not pass away from Me, except I drink it, Thy will be done." Hoping again for human comfort, He sought out His disciples, but found them still sleeping.

Returning to His place of prayer, He falls dying to the ground. This time His prayer is in complete surrender to His Father's will. "If this cup may not pass away from Me, except I drink it, Thy will be done" (Matt. 26:42).

> In this awful crisis, when everything was at stake, when the mysterious cup trembled in the hand of the sufferer, the heavens opened, a light shone forth amid the stormy darkness of the crisis hour, and the mighty angel who stands in God's presence, occupying the position from which Satan fell, came to the side of Christ. The angel came not to take the cup from Christ's hand, but to strengthen Him to drink it, with the assurance of the Father's love. He came to give power to the divine-human suppliant. (White, *The Desire of Ages*, p. 693)

As the light of the divine visitant faded away, Jesus rose from the ground and stood erect. He heard in the distance the sound of a rabble crowd, and saw the flickering lights of torches approaching. Strengthened and comforted by the knowledge of His Father's love, He went forth to meet them.

Chapter 10

The Victory

A strange and unusual darkness covered the hill called Golgotha that day. Jesus had been placed upon a cross and hung between two thieves at around nine o'clock that morning. But by noon, His agony and suffering had increased, and the darkness descended like a cloak around Him as though to shield His last hours from the gaze of the multitude who congregated around the base of the three crosses. Now and then a shaft of lightening slashed through the clouds. Low moans escaped from the lips of the three dying men. The suffering of Jesus was not so much from His physical pain, but sprang from His sense of separation from the Father.

> The withdrawal of the divine countenance from the Savior in this hour of supreme anguish pierced His heart with a sorrow that can never be fully understood by man. So great was His agony that His physical pain was hardly felt. (White, *The Desire of Ages*, p. 753)

Suddenly Jesus cried out in a loud voice, "My God, my God, why have you forsaken me?" Angels veiled their faces from the awful scene. Women wept. Some who were passing by wagged their heads and said, "So! You who are going to destroy the temple and build it in three days, come down from the cross and save yourself! He saved others, but He can't save Himself! Let this Christ, this

King of Israel, come down now from the cross, that we may see and believe" (Mark 15:29–32).

Could the heavens have parted, and the eyes of the careless crowd have been opened to the cosmic realities of what was taking place, all would have fallen on their faces in terror.

> God and His holy angels were beside the cross. The Father was with His Son. Yet His presence was not revealed. Had His glory flashed forth from the cloud, every human beholder would have been destroyed. And in that dreadful hour Christ was not to be comforted with the Father's presence. He trod the wine press alone, and of the people there was none with Him. (White, *The Desire of Ages*, pp. 753, 754)

> God and the angels clothed themselves with darkness, and hid the Savior from the gaze of the curious multitude while He drank the last dregs of the cup of God's wrath.... The angels suffered with Christ. God Himself was crucified with Christ; for Christ was One with the Father. (*The SDA Bible Commentary,* vol. 5, p. 1108)

> In silence the beholders watched for the end of the fearful scene. The sun shone forth; but the cross was still enveloped in darkness. Priests and rulers looked toward Jerusalem; and lo, the dense cloud had settled over the city and the plains of Judea. The Sun of Righteousness, the Light of the world, was withdrawing His beams from the once favored city of Jerusalem. The fierce lightnings of God's wrath were directed against the fated city.

Suddenly the gloom lifted from the cross, and in clear, trumpet-like tones…Jesus cried, "It is finished." "Father, into Thy hands I commend My spirit." A light encircled the cross, and the face of the Savior shone with a glory like the sun. He then bowed His head upon His breast, and died.

Amid the awful darkness, apparently forsaken of God, Christ had drained the last dregs in the cup of human woe. In those dreadful hours he had relied upon the evidence of His Father's acceptance heretofore given Him. He was acquainted with the character of His Father; He understood His justice, His mercy, and His great love. By faith He rested in Him whom it had ever been His joy to obey. And as in submission He committed Himself to God, the sense of His Father's favor was withdrawn. By faith, Christ was victor. (White, *The Desire of Ages*, p. 756)

At that very moment, the veil in the temple that separated the holy and most holy places was rent in two by an unseen hand. It was the time of the evening sacrifice, but in the subsequent terror and confusion, the officiating priest dropped the knife, and the lamb escaped. Type had met antitype in the death of the Savior. The way into the holiest was laid open. No longer did sinful humanity need to look to an earthly high priest for reconciliation with God.

Henceforth the Savior was to officiate as priest and advocate in the heaven of heavens…. "By His own blood" He entereth "in once into the holy place, having obtained eternal redemption for us." (Ibid., p. 757)

There was confusion in the ranks of the enemy after Jesus closed His eyes in death. Throughout Jesus' life on earth they had tried every evil art they knew to cause Him to sin, but He never yielded to their wiles for even one moment. They had thrown every temptation known to man into His pathway, but nothing proved successful. After each skirmish with Him, they were forced to retire from the battle in humiliation and defeat. But Satan felt sure that as Jesus hung on the cross, separated from His Father's influence and protection, he would be able to conquer at last. He required every evil angel in his kingdom to be stationed at the cross. Everything he and his hosts had fought to gain would be lost if they failed in the last few hours of Jesus' life on earth.

As Jesus breathed His last, Satan knew that his hopes of absolute victory over the kingdom of heaven were crushed. But when he saw the precious body of the Lord lying in the tomb, his hopes rose again. If he could just keep Jesus his prisoner under the power of death, he could still win the battle! He gathered his hosts around the tomb, and waited as Jesus rested over the Sabbath hours, according to the commandment.

Early on Sunday morning, there was a violent earthquake, and a mighty angel descended from heaven, rolled back the stone that covered the mouth of the cave where Jesus lay, and with a powerful voice he cried, "Son of God, come forth; your Father calls You!" As Jesus came out of the tomb, He came not in weakness and humiliation, but in majesty and glory as a mighty conqueror; and the angel host bowed low in adoration before the Redeemer, and welcomed Him with songs of praise (Ibid., p. 780). Satan's hopes of victory over the Son of God were vanquished. He would now turn all his efforts toward winning the allegiance of God's people to his side through persecution and deceit.

"... Now have come the salvation and the power and the kingdom of our God, and the authority of His Christ ... Therefore rejoice, you heavens and you who dwell in them! But woe to

the earth and the sea, because the devil has gone down to you!
He is filled with fury, because he knows that his time is short"
(Rev. 12:10, 12).

Chapter 11

The Outpouring

Although longing to visit His Father, Jesus lingered in the garden near the tomb, knowing that His disciples and closest friends would soon visit the site of His burial to grieve, and to prepare His body with spices. Two angels stayed with Him to announce the joyful news that Jesus had risen, just as He had told them He would. As the various groups arrived, the angels tried to help them understand the meaning of the empty tomb, but it all seemed so confusing and hard for them to comprehend. When the women ran to report the angels' words to the apostles, they did not believe their testimony because it seemed like nonsense to them (Luke 24:9–11). Finally all of them went back to their homes (John 20:10).

But Mary Magdalene could not be consoled in her grief. Her Best Friend, her benefactor, Her Savior and Lord was dead! And now even His body had disappeared. She missed Him so terribly that she felt as though her heart was about to break. Where could He be? Why had someone taken His body away? Looking into the tomb, she saw the two angels, but even that did not console her. It was Jesus that she was seeking; no one else could take His place. Intending to go out into the garden, she turned from the tomb and saw a man standing nearby.

"'Woman,' he said, 'why are you crying? Who is it that you are looking for?'" (John 20:15).

"Oh, sir," she replied, "I am seeking Jesus, the man who was crucified on Friday and laid in this very tomb. But now He is gone, and I don't know where to find Him!"

"Mary!" He said, in the gentle voice she knew so well. At once she recognized Him, and falling at His feet, she reached out to touch Him.

"Mary, do not hold on to Me, for I have not yet returned to My Father. But go to My disciples and tell them that I am going to My Father and your Father, and to My God and your God" (John 20:17).

Only then did He make the swift journey to heaven to receive the approval of His Father and the confirmation that His work on earth had accomplished their goal of providing salvation for every descendent of Adam who would accept His sacrifice and live his life by the power of the Holy Spirit.

By evening, Jesus had returned from the joyful but brief reunion with His Father, and entered the room in which His disciples had locked themselves for fear of the Jewish leaders.

"Peace, be with you!" He said. "As the Father has sent me, I am sending you." Then He breathed on them and said, "Receive the Holy Spirit" (John 20:21, 22).

During the 40 days that Jesus stayed with His disciples after His resurrection, He visited them numerous times. They were still so dull in their comprehension of the meaning of Christ's life. They were so accustomed to the teachings of the scribes and Pharisees and leaders of the Jewish nation that the real truth about God and His eternal plan of salvation was almost entirely lost. By His life and teachings for the three and a half years of His ministry, He had endeavored to open their minds to a new way of understanding. But not until He died and rose again could their minds begin to grasp the enormity of what had transpired.

On the walk to Emmaus with two of His disciples, Jesus said to them, "How foolish you are, and how slow of heart to believe all that the prophets have spoken! ... And beginning with Moses and all the Prophets, he explained to them what was said in all the Scriptures concerning himself" (Luke 24:25, 27).

On another occasion, He explained to those who were present, "This is what I told you while I was still with you: Everything must be fulfilled that is written about me in the Law of Moses, the Prophets, and the Psalms. Then he opened their minds so they could understand the Scriptures" (Luke 24:44, 45).

In the centuries before Jesus came to earth, the plan of salvation remained obscure. Animal sacrifices could not give a clear picture of the love, character and law of God. The Sanctuary was a symbolic ritual of better things to come. Its true meaning could only be explained in the light of Jesus' life on earth and His continuing ministry in heaven. The full understanding would only be revealed as the centuries rolled by and other truths became open for the study of God's people. Many things would be revealed after the disciples had gone to their rest, for the truth of God is continually expanding, ever more until that perfect day when Jesus returns (Prov. 4:18).

Thus, Jesus explained to the disciples only that which they needed to know to sweep away the errors and misconceptions of the meaning of the sacrificial system which pointed forward to the coming of the Messiah. He would not reign as an earthly king, as they had been taught. He would reign in majesty as King of kings and Lord of lords only after the full light of His gospel, and the knowledge of His character and law were completely made clear to all inhabitants of earth.

His predictions of His second coming brought joy and hope to the hearts of His disciples and followers, but they had no concept of the passing of time and the experience of His church before that time arrived. Satan must be allowed to display the outworking of the principles of his kingdom so completely that not one soul would ever again be tempted to question God's wisdom in requiring obedience to the laws of His government. It would be seen that these laws are for the protection, happiness and freedom of all His created beings.

After Jesus ascended to heaven to begin His work as Mediator for His people, He sent the gift of His Holy Spirit, manifested as tongues of fire upon their heads. This represented the continuing enlightenment and power they would need to accomplish the monumental task of spreading the gospel to the world in their generation, as Jesus had commissioned them before His ascension (Matt. 28:18-20; see Appendix 1, Christ's Heavenly Ministry).

> When Christ passed within the heavenly gates He was enthroned amidst the adoration of the angels. As soon as this ceremony was completed, the Holy Spirit descended upon the disciples in rich currents, and Christ was indeed glorified, even with the glory which He had with the Father from all eternity. (White, *The Acts of the Apostles*, pp. 38, 39)

> But after Christ's ascension His enthronement in His mediatorial kingdom was signalized by the outpouring of the Holy Spirit. (White, *Christ's Object Lessons*, p. 120)

> God has raised this Jesus to life, and we are all witnesses of the fact. Exalted to the right hand of God, he has received from the Father the promised Holy Spirit and has poured out what you now see and hear. (Acts 2:32, 33)

The precious gift of the Comforter, the Holy Spirit that Jesus had promised them (John 14:25–29), kept them in constant

connection with the throne room in heaven, where Jesus minis-
tered for them. Never were they absent from His love and care.
And the Christian church prospered and grew in spite of all Satan's
efforts to stop its progress by persecution and hardship.

Chapter 12

The Final Generation

After the deaths of the apostles of Jesus, Satan had more control of the minds of the people. Before several centuries had passed, an amalgamation of Christianity and paganism began to develop. But this had all been predicted by Jesus both in His earthly ministry, and especially His heavenly ministry through His beloved disciple, John. Banished to the isle of Patmos, John was given the most astounding revelations of the work of Jesus as High Priest from the time of His ascension until His return to earth in majesty and glory to receive His cleansed and pure bride and take her home to be with Him forever.

These revelations were given and written down in code language so that only with the enlightenment of the Holy Spirit could they be correctly deciphered and understood. This was to protect and guard the truth contained there until the time for them to be opened to the generation of God's people to whom they would apply. In this way, Satan, his fallen angelic hosts, and his earthly followers would not be able to discern God's plan ahead of time, and thus prepare a plan of attack to thwart what God would do at the appointed time.

With each passing generation, the darkness deepened, until the 1260 years predicted by both Daniel and John were fulfilled (Dan. 7:25 and 12:7; Rev. 11:2; 12:14). Historians estimate that fifty million

Christians died for their faith during those long, dark centuries of persecution, now called the Dark Ages. Only the loving, sustaining ministry of Jesus in the heavenly Sanctuary for them, sending light and strength to them through His Spirit and through His Word, kept the faith of these precious souls alive during that time. That is why Daniel was shown in prophetic vision that Satan, through the little horn power that represented him, cast the truth of the ministry of Jesus in the heavenly Sanctuary to the ground, and substituted his own priests on earth who claimed to absolve sin (Dan. 8:9–12). Thus, Satan hoped to obliterate the truth that Jesus had opened the way for every person to have free access to the Father in heaven if they would come by faith in Jesus.

Although it seemed that the great majority of people were deceived by this counterfeit system of worship, God's true and faithful followers never lost sight of their Lord. As a spectacle to the universe, they endured the worst onslaughts of the evil one, and persevered by faith, even to death, rather than be separated from their precious Savior, just as He had done for them on the cross of Calvary.

"They overcame him by the blood of the Lamb and by the word of their testimony; they did not love their lives so much as to shrink from death" (Rev. 12:11).

But Satan learns from experience, too, just like all of us. He saw that persecution only heightened the determination of Christ's followers to stand firm and faithful at all cost to themselves. So he devised another plan. Worldly pleasures and association with unbelievers was always successful to his cause. In the time of Noah, the people were seduced by beauty, wealth, leisure, and fleshly attractions (*The SDA Bible Commentary,* vol. 1, p. 1088), until every inclination of the thoughts of their hearts were only evil all the time (Gen. 6:5). And God was grieved that He had made them (verse 8), for the earth was corrupt and full of violence (verse 11).

Sodom and Gomorra, Rome, and many other nations and societies throughout history have demonstrated that pleasure, ease, and popularity win more people to the side of Satan than do the rack and the stake. And so, when the 1260 years of persecution came to an end, the era of industry, wealth, inventions and power began. Slowly at first, and then more and more rapidly until the world today would be completely baffling to any generation who has gone before us.

But this, too, was predicted by God in prophecy:

> But thou, O Daniel, shut up the words, and seal
> the book, even to the time of the end: many shall
> run to and fro, and knowledge shall be increased.
> (Dan. 12:4, KJV)

It does not take a lot of guessing to pinpoint the time of history that Daniel is speaking about. Looking down through the centuries, God predicted our time and place in the stream of history. We are now on stage, and our destiny depends upon how we represent the King of Heaven as He asks us to step up and be counted for Him.

Consider with me some of the challenges we are currently facing. In most countries around the world, methods of communication and travel have transformed us into a global society, imbibing in the same concepts of modern culture and thought, and seeing life from a similar standpoint. Through personal media, we can be in instant contact with anyone else around the world. Because of this, there has inevitably become a merging of thought, attitudes, and beliefs derived from all cultures, religions, and ideologies. If all religions and ideologies were based upon the eternal truths of God's Word, this would be a positive thing. But that is not the case.

Satan claims to be the Prince of the kingdoms of this world (Matt. 4:8), and therefore, everything coming from the world is a mixture of the principles of good and evil, taken directly from the forbidden tree in the Garden of Eden. Furthermore, Satan is becoming much more adept at deception than he was back at the tree. He has practiced his arts for thousands of years, and he has learned all too well how to appeal to the human heart. No matter how much we think we know about the nature of sin, we are no match for his wiles unless we have the power of the Holy Spirit indwelling our lives.

Unfortunately, modern Christianity has also has become infected with the society in which we live. It has always been the tendency for God's people to assimilate over time to the lifestyle of the world around them. The profligacy before the flood, the apostasy of the Israelite nation, and the amalgamation of the Christian church with the pagans around them during the Dark Ages, are all examples and warnings of how easy it is to slip into compromise with the lifestyle and beliefs of those around us.

The Laodicean church, which is last of the seven churches listed in Revelation 3:14–22, is characterized as "lukewarm" by Jesus. He cautions them to buy of Him gold tried in the fire, eye salve, and white raiment. Obviously they too have fallen into a comfortable state of religion that allows both hot and cold—good and evil—to be mixed in their religious life. This condition which seems so comfortable, so righteous, and so safe is a fatal deception, for the result is that unless the admonition of Jesus is heeded, He will cease to plead His blood for them before the throne of His Father (verse 16), for they do not represent Him in life and practice. Like Lot's wife, their affections have imperceptibly become more in tune with the earthly society to which they have grown to be accustomed, than to the society of the holy angels who seek to draw their attention to heavenly things. Terrible will be the disappointment of those who have departed from God's law—His covenant of love—and have substituted Satan's counterfeits in their lives! Like ancient Israel, the church of God today must not slip into a state of compromise with the evil around them!

> Know therefore that the LORD your God is God;
> he is the faithful God, keeping his covenant of love
> to a thousand generations of those who love and
> serve him and keep his commands.... If you pay
> attention to these laws and are careful to follow
> them, then the LORD your God will keep his cov-
> enant of love with you, as he swore to your forefa-
> thers.... You will be blessed more than any other
> people.... The LORD will keep you free from every
> disease. He will not inflict on you the horrible dis-
> eases you knew in Egypt, but he will inflict them on
> all who hate you. You must destroy all the peoples
> the LORD your God gives over to you. Do not look
> on them with pity and do not serve their gods, for
> they will be a snare to you. (Deut. 7:9–16)

> But mark this: There will be terrible times in the
> last days. People will be lovers of themselves, lovers
> of money, boastful, proud, abusive, disobedient to
> their parents, ungrateful, unholy, without love, un-
> forgiving, slanderous, without self-control, brutal,
> not lovers of the good, treacherous, rash, conceit-
> ed, lovers of pleasure rather than lovers of God—
> having a form of godliness but denying its power.
> Have nothing to do with them. (2 Tim. 3:1–5)

God's command to His people has always been the same: Stay
away from anything or anyone who would lead us into believing
and indulging in the temptations of the evil one. Adam and Eve
disobeyed that command and fell into the sin that has resulted in
the thousands of years of suffering and death which mankind has

experienced. Through Christ, a way is provided to once more enter through the gate of the lost Eden. But the gate will be closed to those who are not in harmony with God's law and the principles of His government.

Friend, how is it with you and your family? Do the angels love to dwell in your home, where all is peace and unselfish love? Or is there arguing and criticism, blaming and alienation which cause the angels of God to veil their faces and weep? What kind of music and entertainment is in your home? Does your clothing represent the pure covering given by God to Adam and Eve, or the scanty fig leaves fashioned to cover their nakedness?

In the home and in the church, God's faithful last generation people are called to reflect the finished work of salvation that Jesus has provided for us.

> Make every effort to live in peace with all men and to be holy; without holiness no one will see the Lord. (Heb. 12:14)

But what is holiness, and is it an attainable goal while here on this earth? Ellen White defines holiness as, "agreement with God" (White, *Testimonies for the Church,* vol. 5, p. 743)

> If man is to become immortal, he must be in harmony with God's mind. (White, *Testimonies on Sexual Behavior, Adultery, and Divorce*, p. 116)

This idea is further cemented in the following passage.

> Do not be yoked together with unbelievers. For what do righteousness and wickedness have in common? Or what fellowship can light have with darkness? What harmony is there between Christ

and Belial? Or what does a believer have in common with an unbeliever? What agreement is there between the temple of God and idols? For we are the temple of the living God. As God has said, "I will live with them and walk among them, and I will be their God, and they will be my people." "Therefore come out from them and be separate," says the Lord. "Touch no unclean thing, and I will receive you. I will be a Father to you and you will be my sons and daughters," says the Lord Almighty. (2 Cor. 6:14–18)

As we consider the perfect plan of God for the creation of mankind, modeled after the loving relationship of the members of the Godhead itself, how cheap are the emotions that we sometimes call love here on this earth. How fickle and selfish they often are. Sin is no longer sin if it satisfies my needs; rebellion is no longer rebellion if it helps me reach my goals. It has become fashionable to redefine God's law to suit my human condition. But this flies in the face of all that God has done to provide restitution and reconciliation through His Son. Did He die only to allow the sinners back into heaven whose lives are not completely cleansed from the seeds of the rebellion that Lucifer began in heaven?

No, my friend, sin will be completely eradicated by the precious blood of Jesus! Before His ministry in the heavenly sanctuary comes to a close, His work must produce in His faithful followers upon earth a bride who is in full harmony with every principle of His law of love.

… Christ loved the church and gave himself up for her to make her holy, cleansing her by the washing with water through the word, and to present her to himself as a radiant church, without stain or

wrinkle or any other blemish, but holy and blameless. (Eph. 5:25–27)

Sin began through disagreement with God's principles and rebellion against His law; sin will end when complete understanding
and harmony is restored. Some believe that this will not take place
until we receive immortal bodies at the coming of Christ. But perfect bodies do not guarantee perfect minds, as has already been
proven by Lucifer's defection and Adam's fall. God gives created
beings the right to choose what direction their thoughts will take.
Although the carnal nature with which we were born is naturally
at enmity with God's law and cannot be subject to it (Rom. 8:7),
Jesus abolished the enmity through His death on the cross (Eph.
2:15, 16) by displaying the true nature of His Father, and providing
a way back into favor and reconciliation with God. Harmony with
God and obedience to His law is a result of a close and constant
walk with Jesus through the indwelling of His Spirit; and this is
available to everyone as long as Jesus' ministry in the heavenly
sanctuary continues.

But the time will come when everyone will be called to make
their final decisions for or against God and His law. Through the
centuries God has been preparing His church for the full display of His grace in the final generation. Those who have prepared for that time by cleansing their hearts from all earthly lusts
(James 4:1–10), will receive the full outpouring of His Spirit. As
the former rain was poured out moderately at Pentecost at the
inauguration of His ministry (Joel 2:23), so the latter rain will be
a sign from Jesus that His work in the heavenly sanctuary is completed, and that His people have been cleansed from all sympathy
with sin (1 Peter 4:1, 2).

And afterward, I will pour out my Spirit on all people. Your sons and daughters will prophesy, your

old men will dream dreams, your young men will
see visions. Even on my servants, both men and
women, I will pour out my Spirit in those days. I
will show wonders in the heavens and on the earth,
blood and fire and billows of smoke. The sun will
be turned to darkness and the moon to blood before the coming of the great and dreadful day of
the Lord. And everyone who calls on the name of
the Lord will be saved; for on Mount Zion and in
Jerusalem there will be deliverance, as the Lord
has said, even among the survivors [remnant,
KJV] whom the Lord calls. (Joel 2:28–32)

Through God's final people, the inhabitants of the world will
be permitted to see what Jesus' sacrifice and heavenly ministry can
produce in human lives. With faces glowing with glory from heav-
en (Isa. 60:1–3; 62:1–3), they will preach the last warning message
from heaven.

With a mighty voice he shouted: Fallen! Fallen is Babylon the
Great! She has become a home for demons and a haunt for every evil spirit, a haunt for every unclean and detestable bird. For
all nations have drunk the maddening wine of her adulteries…
Come out of her, my people, so that you will not share in her
sins, so that you will not receive any of her plagues; for her sins
are piled up to heaven, and God has remembered her crimes.
(Rev. 18:2–5)

The imminent destruction of the wicked is implied in this dire
warning. But according to God's own law, no one is to be con-
demned to death on the testimony of only one witness (Deut. 17:6;
see Appendix 2, Second Witnessing).

This eternal principle of the necessity of a second witness has
always been in effect, even before sin. It is the essence of the relationship of love that exists between God and His Son.

> You judge by human standards; I pass judgment
> on no one. But if I do judge, my decisions are right,
> because I am not alone. I stand with the Father,
> who sent me. In your own Law it is written that the
> testimony of two men is valid. I am one who testi-
> fies for myself; my other witness is the Father, who
> sent me. (John 8:15–19)

It is the same relationship that He wants to share with His
bride, the church.

> Now this is eternal life: that they may know you,
> the only true God, and Jesus Christ, whom you
> have sent. I have brought you glory on earth by
> completing the work you gave me to do. And now,
> Father, glorify me in your presence with the glory
> I had with you before the world began... I have re-
> vealed you to those whom you gave me out of the
> world... I have given them the glory that you gave
> me, that they may be one as we are one: I in them
> and you in me. May they be brought to complete
> unity to let the world know that you sent me and
> have loved them even as you have loved me... I
> have made you known to them, and will continue
> to make you known in order that the love you have
> for me may be in them and that I myself may be in
> them. (John 17:3, 6, 22, 23, 26)

This witness is completed in the final generation, for it is their
example that will testify to the justice of God in the destruction of

the wicked. The ripened harvest of both good and evil will be fully displayed, and both sides of the controversy will reap what they and their forebears have sown.

> Woe to you, because you build tombs for the prophets, and it was your forefathers who killed them. So you testify [or witness] that you approve of what your forefathers did; they killed the prophets, and you build their tombs. Because of this, God in His wisdom said, "I will send them prophets and apostles, some of whom they will kill and others they will persecute." Therefore this generation will be held responsible for the blood of all the prophets that has been shed since the beginning of the world... Yes, I tell you, this generation will be held responsible for it all. (Luke 11:47–51)

This is the generation to which we have come. This is the time when final decisions must be made. Soon the conflict of the ages will be upon us.

> Proclaim this among the nations: Prepare for war! ... "Let the nations be roused; let them advance into the Valley of Jehoshaphat, for there I will sit to judge all the nations on every side. Swing the sickle, for the harvest is ripe. Come, trample the grapes, for the winepress is full and the vats overflow—so great is their wickedness!" Multitudes, multitudes in the valley of decision! For the day of the LORD is near in the valley of decision... The LORD will roar from Zion and thunder from Jerusalem; the earth and the sky will tremble. But the LORD will be a refuge for His people, a stronghold for the people

of Israel. (Joel 3:9–16)

As the clouds are gathering on the horizon of this earth, Jesus is making a final call to His people:

> Come, my people, enter your rooms, and shut the doors behind you; hide yourselves for a little while until His wrath has passed by. See, the LORD is coming out of His dwelling to punish the people of the earth for their sins. The earth will disclose the blood shed upon her; she will conceal her slain no longer. (Isa. 26:20, 21; see also Rev. 15 and 16)

> What are the chambers in which they are to hide? They are the protection of Christ and holy angels. (*The SDA Bible Commentary*, vol. 4, p. 1143)

Dear Friend, are you longing to be ready for Jesus' coming but are struggling with some problems in your life that seem to be insurmountable? Are there sins that you do not know how to overcome? If so, reach up and grasp Jesus' hand by faith, for in Him the victory is sure. Your life, too, can be an example to others that Jesus can fully cleanse from sin and live out His life in everyone who will come to Him and receive His Spirit. May these passages of Scripture bring hope to you! May your walk with Jesus grow more precious every day as you heed the call of His Spirit to prepare for His coming.

> "Is anything too hard for the LORD?" (Gen. 18:14a)

> "Come now, let us reason together," says the LORD. "Though your sins are like scarlet, they shall be as white as snow; though they are red as crimson, they

shall be like wool. If you are willing and obedient, you will eat the best from the land; but if you resist and rebel, you will be devoured by the sword." For the mouth of the LORD has spoken. (Isa. 1:18–20)

Nothing impure will ever enter it, nor will anyone who does what is shameful or deceitful, but only those whose names are written in the Lamb's book of life. (Rev. 21:27)

Blessed are those who wash their robes that they may have the right to the tree of life and may go through the gates into the city. (Rev. 22:14)

Then I looked, and there before me was the Lamb, standing on Mt. Zion, and with Him 144,000 who had His name and His Father's name written on their foreheads... They were purchased from among men and offered as firstfruits to God and the Lamb. No lie was found in their mouths. They are blameless. (Rev. 14:1, 4, 5)

Then I heard what sounded like a great multitude, like the roar of rushing waters and like loud peals of thunder, shouting: "Hallelujah! For our Lord God Almighty reigns. Let us rejoice and be glad and give Him glory! For the wedding of the Lamb has come, and His bride has made herself ready. Fine linen, bright and clean, was given her to wear." [Fine linen stands for the righteous acts of the saints.] Then the angel said to me, "Write: "Blessed are those who are invited to the wedding supper of the Lamb!" (Rev. 19:6–9)

On that day you will not be put to shame for all the wrongs you have done to me, because I will remove from this city those who rejoice in their pride. Never again will you be haughty on my holy hill. But I will leave within you the meek and humble who trust in the name of the LORD. The remnant of Israel will do no wrong; they will speak no lies, nor will deceit be found in their mouths. They will eat and lie down and no one will make them afraid ... At that time I will gather you; at that time I will take you home. (Zeph. 3:11–13, 20)

Epilogue

As Jesus was sitting on the Mount of Olives one day, the disciples came to Him and asked Him to tell them the signs of His second coming. In response to their questions, Jesus outlined the major events that would precede His coming. Recorded in Matthew 24, Mark 13 and Luke 21, He predicted wars, earthquakes, famines, hurricanes, trouble and fear in society, and eventually persecution of His people. But He bade them not to fear.

> They will lay hands on you and persecute you. They will deliver you to synagogues and prison, and you will be brought before kings and governors, and all on account of my name. This will result in your being witnesses to them. But make up your mind not to worry beforehand how you will defend yourselves. For I will give you words and wisdom that none of your adversaries will be able to resist or contradict. You will be betrayed even by parents, brothers, relatives and friends, and they will put some of you to death. All men will hate you because of me. But not a hair of your head will perish. By standing firm you will gain life ...
>
> There will be signs in the sun, moon and stars. On the earth, nations will be in anguish and perplexity at the roaring and tossing of the sea. Men

will faint from terror, apprehensive of what is coming on the world, for the heavenly bodies will be shaken. At that time they will see the Son of Man coming in a cloud with power and great glory. When these things begin to take place, stand up and lift up your heads, because your redemption is drawing near ... When you see these things happening, you know that the kingdom of God is near. I tell you the truth, this generation will certainly not pass away until all these things have happened...

Be careful, or your hearts will be weighed down with dissipation, drunkenness and the anxieties of life, and that day will close on you unexpectedly like a trap ... Be always on the watch, and pray that you may be able to escape all that is about to happen, and that you may be able to stand before the Son of Man. (Luke 21:12–36)

Generations have come and gone since Jesus spoke these words to His disciples, and there has been much trouble in society, in the world, and for God's people through the centuries. Persecution and death stalked those who clung to God and His truth. But the blessed hope of Jesus' coming burned in the heart of every true believer and buoyed them up to bravely face the onslaughts of the enemy. Their thoughts were set on a better world to come, and they lived and died in the faith of the victory that was yet to come. With this caliber of men and women who have gone before us, what is it that God is waiting for? Is there a clock in heaven that still has to count down the minutes of time? Has He not finished going through the books of record? Or is the character quality of His followers the deciding factor in the timing of His return?

> These were all commended for their faith, yet
> none of them received what had been promised.
> God had planned something better for us so that
> only together with us would they be made perfect.
> (Heb. 11:39, 40)

In other words, the plan of salvation is not complete until there is a finished product of the life and ministry of Christ, showing that His grace is sufficient to put an end to sin and sinning. Jesus is the Author and Finisher of our faith. He does not start something that He cannot finish. He did not die on the cross of Calvary until every last particle of His work was done. Then He cried out, "It is finished!" and bowing His head, He committed His spirit into His Father's hands. Likewise, He will not end the great controversy until His work for His people is finished and until they are in complete harmony and agreement with Him.

> Therefore, since we are surrounded by such a great
> cloud of witnesses, let us throw off everything that
> hinders and the sin that so easily entangles, and
> let us run with perseverance the race marked out
> for us. Let us fix our eyes on Jesus, the Author
> and Perfecter of our faith, who for the joy set be-
> fore Him endured the cross, scorning its shame,
> and sat down at the right hand of the throne of
> God. Consider Him who endured such opposition
> from sinful men, so that you will not grow weary
> and lose heart. In your struggle against sin, you
> have not yet resisted to the point of shedding your
> blood. (Heb. 12:1–4)

Everyone who will enter the kingdom of God will develop a character that is the counterpart of the character of God. None can dwell with God in the holy heaven but those who bear His likeness. Those who are to be redeemed are to be overcomers; for they are to be elevated, pure, one with Christ. (*The SDA Bible Commentary,* vol. 6, p. 1105)

Those who reach this condition will be those who have cooperated with Jesus through every part of His sanctuary ministry, including the final cleansing of the heart and mind in the Most Holy Place. They will have listened to His voice of correction and responded to Him on every level.

> Our fathers disciplined us for a little while as they thought best; but God disciplines us for our good, that we may share in His holiness. No discipline seems pleasant at the time, but painful. Later on, however, it produces a harvest of righteousness and peace for those who have been trained by it... Make every effort to live in peace with all men and to be holy; without holiness no one will see the Lord. (Heb. 12:10, 11, 14)

Since holiness is agreement with God (White, *Testimonies for the Church,* vol. 5, p. 743), our specific trials will be designed to help us to see any area in which we are in disagreement with God. Do we live in an attitude of praise? Do we esteem others better than ourselves? Do we live by every word that proceeds out of the mouth of God? Are we filled with the character aspects of the Spirit — love, joy, peace, and so on? Does our daily life represent Jesus accurately? Do we have a dynamic prayer life? Do we commune with God moment by moment as did Enoch? (See sanctuary steps in Appendix 2.) If so, we will receive the latter rain of the Holy Spirit and be fitted to follow Jesus through the time of trouble that immediately precedes His coming.

For a moment, let us draw the curtain aside and view the experience of God's people during the final events of earth's history until Jesus comes. The following word pictures come from the pen of Ellen White.

> While Jesus had been ministering in the sanctuary, the judgment had been going on for the righteous dead, and then for the righteous living. Christ had received His kingdom, having made the atonement for His people and blotted out their sins. The subjects of the kingdom were made up. The marriage of the Lamb was consummated ...
>
> As Jesus moved out of the most holy place... a cloud of darkness covered the inhabitants of the earth. There was then no mediator between guilty man and an offended God....
>
> Then I saw Jesus lay off His priestly attire and clothe Himself with His most kingly robes.... Surrounded by the angelic host, He left heaven.... Now there was no atoning blood to cleanse the guilty, no compassionate Savior to plead for them, and cry, 'Spare, spare the sinner a little longer.' All heaven had united with Jesus, as they heard the fearful words, 'It is done. It is finished.' The plan of salvation had been accomplished, but few had chosen to accept it. (White, *Early Writings*, pp. 280, 281)

> As the saints left the cities and villages, they were pursued by the wicked, who sought to slay them. But the swords that were raised to kill God's people broke and fell as powerless as a straw. Angels of God shielded the saints. As they cried day and

night for deliverance, their cry came up before the Lord....

Soon appeared the great white cloud, upon which sat the Son of man. When it first appeared in the distance, this cloud looked very small.... As it drew nearer the earth, we could behold the excellent glory and majesty of Jesus as He rode forth to conquer. A retinue of holy angels, with bright, glittering crowns upon their heads, escorted Him on His way. No language can describe the glory of the scene. The living cloud of majesty and unsurpassed glory came still nearer, and we could clearly behold the lovely person of Jesus. He did not wear a crown of thorns, but a crown of glory rested upon His holy brow. Upon His vesture and thigh was a name written, King of kings, and Lord of lords. His countenance was as bright as the noonday sun, His eyes were as a flame of fire, and his feet had the appearance of fine brass. His voice sounded like many musical instruments....

The earth mightily shook as the voice of the Son of God called forth the sleeping saints. They responded to the call and came forth clothed with glorious immortality.... Then the living saints and the risen ones raised their voices in a long, transporting shout of victory.... The living saints are changed in a moment, in the twinkling of an eye, and caught up with the risen ones, and together they meet their Lord in the air. Oh, what a glorious meeting! Friends whom death had separated were united, never more to part. (Ibid., pp. 284–288)

Before the ransomed throng is the holy city. Jesus opens wide the pearly gates, and the nations that have kept the truth enter in. There they behold the Paradise of God, the home of Adam in his innocence. Then that voice, richer than any music that ever fell on mortal ear, is heard, saying, "Your conflict is ended." "Come, ye blessed of My Father, inherit the kingdom prepared for you from the foundation of the world."...

With unutterable love, Jesus welcomes His faithful ones to the "joy of their Lord." The Savior's joy is in seeing, in the kingdom of glory, the souls that have been saved by His agony and humiliation. And the redeemed will be sharers in His joy, as they behold, among the blessed, those who have been won to Christ through their prayers, their labors, and their loving sacrifice ...

As the ransomed ones are welcomed to the city of God, there rings out upon the air an exultant cry of adoration. The two Adams are about to meet. The Son of God is standing with outstretched arms to receive the father of our race—the being whom He created, who sinned against his maker, and for whose sin the marks of the crucifixion are borne upon the Savior's form. As Adam discerns the prints of the cruel nails, he does not fall upon the bosom of his Lord, but in humiliation casts himself at His feet, crying, 'Worthy, worthy is the Lamb that was slain!' Tenderly the Savior lifts him up, and bids him look once more upon the Eden home from which he has so long been exiled....

Transported with joy, he beholds the trees that were once his delight—the very trees whose fruit he himself had gathered in the days of his innocence and joy. He sees the vines that his own hands have trained, the very flowers that he once loved to care for. His mind grasps the reality of the scene; he comprehends that this is indeed Eden restored, more lovely now than when he was banished from it. The Savior leads him to the tree of life, and plucks the glorious fruit, and bids him eat. He looks about him, and beholds a multitude of his family redeemed, standing in the Paradise of God. Then he casts his glittering crown at the feet of Jesus, and falling upon His breast, embraces the Redeemer. He touches the golden harp, and the vaults of heaven echo the triumphant song, "Worthy, worthy, worthy is the Lamb that was slain, and lives again!" The family of Adam take up the strain, and cast their crowns at the Savior's feet as they bow before Him in adoration.

This reunion is witnessed by the angels who wept at the fall of Adam, and rejoiced when Jesus, after His resurrection, ascended to heaven, having opened the grave for all who should believe on His name. Now they behold the work of redemption accomplished, and they unite their voices in the song of praise. (White, *The Great Controversy*, pp. 646–648)

The mystery of the cross explains all other mysteries ... It will be seen that He who is infinite in wisdom could devise no plan for our salvation except the sacrifice of His Son. The compensation for this sacrifice is the joy of peopling the earth with ransomed beings, holy, happy, and immortal. The result of the Savior's conflict with the powers of darkness is joy to the redeemed, redounding to the glory of God throughout eternity. And such is the value of the soul that the Father is satisfied with the price paid; and Christ Himself, beholding the fruits of His great sacrifice, is satisfied. (Ibid., p. 652)

"I saw a new heaven and a new earth: for the first heaven and the first earth were passed away." (Rev. 21:1) ... In the Bible the inheritance of the saved is called a country.... There are ever-flowing streams, clear as crystal, and beside them waving trees cast their shadows upon the paths prepared for the ransomed of the Lord. There the wide-spreading plains swell into hills of beauty, and the mountains of God rear their lofty summits. On those peaceful plains, beside those living streams, God's people, so long pilgrims and wanderers shall find a home. (Ibid., pp. 674, 675)

And the years of eternity, as they roll, will bring richer and still more glorious revelations of God and of Christ. As knowledge is progressive, so will love, reverence, and happiness increase. The more men learn of God, the greater will be their admiration of His character ...

The great controversy is ended. Sin and sinners are no more. The entire universe is clean... From the minutest atom to the greatest world, all things, animate and inanimate, in their unshadowed beauty and perfect joy, declare that God is love. (Ibid., pp. 677, 678)

With these sublime words, the story of the history of sin ends. God's character and His law have been exonerated, and His children rescued. Only one question remains: Where will you and I and our loved ones be when Jesus returns to earth in all His glory to bring His children home? By His grace, we can all be there!

Appendix 1

Christ's Heavenly Ministry

God's purpose has always been to restore heaven and the universe to the original peace and happiness that existed before the defection of Lucifer and his followers. This would necessitate demonstrating to everyone's satisfaction the true motives and character of God and His law. Before Jesus came to earth, the sacrificial system was set up to teach the Israelite nation that God had a plan to remedy the effects of sin in every life through the sanctuary. True believers followed this plan and obeyed its requirements. But when Christ came, the rituals were done away with, for type had met antitype in Jesus, the Lamb that takes away the sins of the world by His life, death, resurrection, and ministry in the heavenly sanctuary. So what can we learn about the divine prescription for the sin problem which is illustrated in the sanctuary?

The first principle to recognize is that the sanctuary is constructed to give us a glimpse into the throne room of God, and learn how to comprehend more clearly the pathway of righteousness. Holiness of mind and thought is broken down into seven steps to demonstrate God's character and how he thinks and feels on every subject. By following these principles, we can come into intimate understanding and fellowship with Him.

Son of man, describe the temple to the people of
Israel, that they may be ashamed of their sins. Let
them consider the plan, and ... make known to
them the design of the temple—its arrangement,
its exits and entrances—its whole design and all
its regulations and laws. Write these down before
them so that they may be faithful to its design and
follow all its regulations. (Ezek. 43:10, 11)

It was Christ who planned the arrangement for
the first earthly tabernacle. He...was the heavenly architect who marked out the plan for the sacred building where His name was to be honored.
(White, *Christ's Object Lessons*, p. 349)

Through the sacrifices and offerings brought to
the earthly sanctuary, the children of Israel were
to lay hold of the merits of a Savior to come. And,
in the wisdom of God, the particulars of this work
were given us that we might, by looking to them,
understand the work of Jesus in the heavenly sanctuary. (White, *Early Writings*, p. 253)

I saw that everything in heaven was in perfect order. Said the angel, 'Behold ye and know how perfect, how beautiful the order in heaven; follow it.
(White, *Early Writings*, pp. xxx, xxxi)

What is this perfect order that we are to follow? Consider be-
low the sanctuary steps of prayer and worship.

Praise

> Enter His gates with thanksgiving and His courts with praise. (Ps. 100:4)

> Jesus said, ... "I am the gate; whoever enters through me will be saved." (John 10:7–9)

> Christ, our Mediator, and the Holy Spirit are constantly interceding in man's behalf, but the Spirit pleads not for us as does Christ who presents His blood ... The Spirit works upon our hearts, drawing out prayers and penitence, praise and thanksgiving. The gratitude which flows from our lips is the result of the Spirit striking the cords of the soul in holy memories, awakening the music of the soul in holy memories, awakening the music of the heart. (White, "Our Great High Priest," *The Youth's Instructor,* April 16, 1903)

> The day is coming in which the battle will have been fought, the victory won... All will be a happy, united family, clothed with the garments of praise and thanksgiving—the robe of Christ's righteousness. (White, *Testimonies for the Church*, vol. 8, p. 42)

Altar of Sacrifice: Repentance, Confession, Humbling of self

> If we confess our sins, He is faithful and just and will forgive us our sins and purify us from all unrighteousness. (1 John 1:9)

Do nothing out of selfish ambition or vain conceit, but in humility consider others better than yourselves. Each of you should look not only to your own interests, but also to the interests of others. Your attitude should be the same as that of Christ Jesus: Who ... did not consider equality with God something to be grasped, but made himself nothing, taking the very nature of a servant,.. he humbled himself and became obedient to death.... Therefore God exalted him to the highest place and gave him the name that is above every name, that at the name of Jesus every knee should bow in heaven and on earth. (Phil. 2:3–10)

Laver: Washed by the Water of the Word

Jesus answered, "It is written: 'Man does not live on bread alone, but on every word that comes from the mouth of God.'" (Matt. 4:4)

Christ loved the church and gave Himself up for her to make her holy, cleansing her by the washing with water through the word, and to present her to Himself as a radiant church, without stain or wrinkle or any other blemish, but holy and blameless. (Eph. 5:25–27)

Appropriating the word to our spiritual necessities is the eating of the leaves of the tree of life that are for the healing of the nations. Study the word, and practice the word, for it is your life. (*Counsels on Sabbath School Work*, p. 44)

Seven-branched Candlestick: The Infilling of the Holy Spirit

I see a solid gold lampstand with a bowl at the top and seven lights on it, with seven channels to the lights ... This is the word of the LORD to Zerubbabel: "Not by might nor by power, but by my Spirit, says the LORD Almighty." (Zech. 4:2, 6)

Before the throne, seven lamps were blazing. These are the seven Spirits of God. (Rev. 4:5)

I pray that out of his glorious riches he may strengthen you with power through his Spirit in your inner being, so that Christ may dwell in your hearts through faith. (Eph. 3:16, 17).

Live by the Spirit and you will not gratify the desires of the sinful nature ... But the fruit of the Spirit is love, joy, peace, patience, kindness, goodness, faithfulness, gentleness and self-control. (Gal. 5:16, 22, 23)

The impartation of the Spirit is the impartation of the life of Christ. It imbues the receiver with the attributes of Christ. (White, *The Desire of Ages*, p. 805)

Table of Shewbread: Symbol of Christ's Life for His People

I am the bread of life ... I am the living bread that came down from heaven. If anyone eats of this bread, he will live forever.... Just as the living Father sent me and I live because of the Father, so the one who feeds on me will live because of me…. The Spirit gives life…. The words that I have spoken to you are Spirit and they are life. (John 6:51, 57, 63)

Study carefully the divine-human character, and constantly inquire, "What would Jesus do if He were in my place?" This should be the measurement of our duty. (White, *The Ministry of Healing*, p. 491)

The Holy Spirit is in the word of God…. He who thus eats the bread of heaven is nourished every day…. Here is presented before us a rich banquet, of which all who believe in Christ as a personal Savior may eat. He is the tree of life to all who continue to feed on Him. (White, *This Day With God*, p. 292)

It is a knowledge of the perfection of the divine character, manifested to us in Jesus Christ, that opens up to us communion with God… Christ must be all in all to us; He must dwell in the heart; His life must circulate through us, as the blood circulates through the veins. (White, *Our High Calling*, p. 60)

God must ever be in our thoughts. We must hold converse with Him while we walk by the way, and while our hands are engaged in labor. In all the purposes and pursuits of life we must inquire, What will the Lord have me to do? How shall I please Him who has given His life a ransom for me? Thus may we walk with God, as did Enoch of old; and ours may be the testimony which he received, that he pleased God. (Ibid., p. 61)

Altar of Incense: The Place of Intercession for One's Self and Others

Another angel, who had a golden censer, came and stood at the altar. He was given much incense to offer, with the prayers of all the saints, on the golden altar before the throne. The smoke of the incense, together with the prayers of the saints, went up before God from the angel's hand. (Rev. 8:3, 4)

May my prayer be set before you like incense; may the lifting up of my hands be like the evening sacrifice. (Ps. 141:2)

The Spirit helps us in our weakness. We do not know what we ought to pray for, but the Spirit himself intercedes for us with groans that words cannot express. And he who searches our hearts knows the mind of the Spirit, because the Spirit intercedes for the saints in accordance with God's will. (Rom. 8:26, 27)

We must not only pray in Christ's name, but by the inspiration of the Holy Spirit ... Such prayer God delights to answer. When with earnestness and intensity we breathe a prayer in the name of Christ, there is in that very intensity a pledge from God that He is about to answer our prayer "exceeding abundantly above all that we ask or think."

Eph. 3:20. (White, *Christ's Object Lessons*, p. 147)

The prayer of the humble suppliant [Christ] pres-
ents as His own desire in that soul's behalf. Every
sincere prayer is heard in heaven. It may not be
fluently expressed; but if the heart is in it, it will
ascend to the sanctuary where Jesus ministers, and
He will present it to the Father without one awk-
ward, stammering word, beautiful and fragrant
with the incense of His own perfection. (White,
Lift Him Up, p. 190)

Morning and evening the heavenly universe beholds every household that prays, and the angel
with the incense, representing the blood of the
atonement, finds access to God. (*The SDA Bible
Commentary*, vol. 7, p. 971)

**The Most Holy Place: The place of Christ's Final Atoning Work
of Judgment; Bringing His People into Full Agreement with His
Holy Law by the Cleansing and Removal of their Sins.**

Then God's temple in heaven was opened, and
within his temple was seen the ark of his covenant.
And there came flashes of lightning, rumblings,
peals of thunder, an earthquake and a great hail-
storm. (Rev. 11:19)

As I looked, thrones were set in place, and the
Ancient of Days took his seat. His clothing was as
white as the snow; the hair of his head was white
like wool. His throne was flaming with fire, and its
wheels were all ablaze. A river of fire was flowing,

coming out from before him. Thousands upon thousands attended him; ten thousand times ten thousand stood before him. The court was seated, and the books were opened. (Dan. 7:9, 10)

In the Old Testament sanctuary service, this day of judgment was prefigured by the yearly Day of Atonement, when the high priest figuratively removed the sins of the people from the sanctuary. All were required to participate or be cut off from the people of God.

> This is to be a lasting ordinance for you: On the tenth day of the seventh month you must deny [afflict] yourselves and not do any work ... because on this day atonement will be made for you to cleanse you. Then, before the LORD, you will be clean from all your sins. (Lev. 16:29, 30)

> Anyone who does not deny [afflict] himself on that day must be cut off from his people. (Lev. 23:29)

The people were to participate through the day by deep searching of heart, and confession of any lingering sins that might be brought up to them by the Spirit of God. This prayer of David is an example of such a prayer:

> Have mercy on me, O God, according to your unfailing love; according to your great compassion blot out my transgressions. Wash away all my iniquity and cleanse me from my sin ... Surely I was sinful at birth, sinful from the time my mother conceived me. Surely you desire truth in the inner parts; you teach me wisdom in the inmost place. Cleanse me

with hyssop, and I will be clean; wash me, and I will be whiter than snow ... Hide your face from my sins and blot out all my iniquity. Create in me a pure heart, O God, and renew a steadfast spirit within me. Do not cast me from your presence or take your Holy Spirit from me. Restore to me the joy of your salvation and grant me a willing spirit to sustain me. Then I will teach transgressors your ways, and sinners will turn back to you. (Ps. 51:1–13)

God's response to His people's sincere repentance and confession is recorded in this scripture: "I will give them an undivided heart and put a new spirit in them; I will remove from them their heart of stone and give them a heart of flesh. Then they will follow my decrees and be careful to keep my laws. They will be my people and I will be their God" (Ezek. 11:19, 20).

All of this prefigured the work of Christ in the heavenly sanctuary:

Therefore, brothers, since we have confidence to enter the Most Holy Place by the blood of Jesus by a new and living way opened for us through the curtain, that is, his body, and since we have a great priest over the house of God, let us draw near to God with a sincere heart in full assurance of faith, having our hearts sprinkled to cleanse us from a guilty conscience... Let us hold unswervingly to the hope we profess, for he who has promised is faithful ... And all the more as you see the Day approaching. (Heb. 10:19–25)

Yes, the final work of Christ just before He comes again, is to produce a people who love Him so much that they will cooperate with Him fully in His work of cleansing sin, root and branch, from their lives.

> The Holy Spirit also testifies to us about this. First He says: "This is the covenant I will make with them after that time, says the Lord. I will put my laws in their hearts, and I will write them on their minds." Then he adds: "Their sins and lawless acts I will remember no more" (Heb. 10:15–17)

> Pressing close to His side and holding communion with Him, we become like Him. Through the transforming power of the Spirit of Christ, we are changed in heart and life. His words are engraved on the tablets of the soul, and we are His witnesses, representing Him in the daily life. (White, *This Day With God*, p. 96)

> From the beginning it has been God's plan that through His church should be reflected to the world His fullness and His sufficiency. The members of His church... are to show forth His glory. The church is the repository of the riches of Christ; and through the church will eventually be made manifest, even to the 'principalities and powers in heavenly places,' the final and full display of the love of God. (White, *The Acts of the Apostles*, p. 9)

At last, Jesus' longing to have His bride eternally with Him in heaven will be satisfied!

> "To him who overcomes, I will give the right to sit with me on my throne, just as I overcame and sat

down with my Father on his throne. He who has an ear, let him hear what the Spirit says to the churches" (Rev. 3:21, 22).

Appendix 2

Second Witnessing

Examples of the principle of second-witnessing are all throughout the Bible. Paul mentions it in 2 Corinthians 13:1–3, when dealing with certain problems in the Corinthian church. Jesus followed this principle with the woman caught in adultery, and set her free when there were no witnesses against her (John 8:1–11). But nowhere is the understanding of this principle more important than in the final generation.

Jesus came to earth to witness of His Father's character of love. But Jesus also needs the witness of His people on earth that His sacrifice is sufficient to restore man completely from the effects of sin.

Therefore, it must be demonstrated that the perfect life Jesus that He lived while on this earth can produce the same character of love and obedience in the lives of His people. There must be a generation of God's people who will fully reject Satan's accusations against the character of God, and come into complete harmony with His law. Thus they will be the second witness needed before the universe that God's dealings with the wicked are just and holy and righteous.

It is this principle that is implied in Christ's injunction to His disciples in Acts 1:8:

But you will receive power when the Holy Spirit comes on you; and you will be my witnesses in Jerusalem, and in all Judea and Samaria, and to the ends of the earth.

Lucifer was given the high position of knowing God and His character and sharing this intimate knowledge with all other created beings. Instead, he used his position to do just the opposite, and defame God's character until he took a third of the angels into rebellion with him.

Eve was created to be the companion of Adam, and by her beautiful life she was to bring honor to his position as head of this earth. In doing this, she would bring glory to him, just as Jesus brings glory to the Father by witnessing to His position as King of the universe, and teaching His principles and exemplifying His character. (Please notice that the robe of light around Adam and Eve did not disappear until Adam second-witnessed her sin, and ate the apple with her [Gen. 3:6, 7].) But we in the human family can still reflect the original purpose for which we were created.

"Now I want you to realize that the head of every man is Christ, and the head of the woman is man, and head of Christ is God... Man is the image and glory of God; but the woman is the glory of man" (1 Cor. 11:3, 7).

Love is the basis of this glory that is given from God the Father to His Son and down to us. And the proper honor that we give to one another is a conduit for the love of God to flow through us to each other, and thus give back to God the glory as it completes the circle. Selfishness interrupts this circle of love, thus those who imbibe in this spirit will not be welcomed into His kingdom.

Bibliography

The New Lexicon Webster's Encyclopedic Dictionary of the English Language. New York: Lexicon Publications, Inc., 1989.

Taber's Cyclopedic Medical Dictionary. 7th edition. Philadelphia: F. A. Davis Co., 1957.

White, Ellen G. *The Acts of the Apostles.* Mountain View, CA: Pacific Press Publishing Association, 1911.

———— "Child Life of Jesus." *The Signs of the Times,* July 30, 1896.

———— "Christ's Ambassadors." *The Review and Herald,* May 29, 1900.

———— *Christ's Object Lessons.* Washington, DC: Review and Herald Publishing Association, 1900.

———— *The Desire of Age.* Mountain View, CA: Pacific Press Publishing Association, 1898.

———— *Early Writings.* Washington, DC: Review and Herald Publishing Association, 1882.

———— *The Faith I Live By.* Washington, DC: Review and Herald Publishing Association, 1958.

———— *The Great Controversy.* Mountain View, CA: Pacific Press Publishing Association, 1911.

———— *Lift Him Up.* Hagerstown, MD: Review and Herald Publishing Association, 1988.

———— "The Liquor Traffic Working Counter to Christ." *The Review and Herald,* May 8, 1894.

————— *Manuscript Releases*. Vol. 11. Silver Spring, MD: Ellen G. White Estate, 1990.

————— *The Ministry of Healing*. Mountain View, CA: Pacific Press Publishing Association, 1905.

————— "The Mystery of God." *The Signs of the Times*, March 25, 1897.

————— "Our Great High Priest." *The Youth's Instructor,* April 16, 1903.

————— *Our High Calling*. Washington, DC: Review and Herald Publishing Association, 1961.

————— *Patriarchs and Prophets*. Washington, DC: Review and Herald Publishing Association, 1890.

————— "Redemption—No. 1." *The Review and Herald,* February 24, 1874.

————— *The SDA Bible Commentary*. Vol. 1. Washington, DC: Review and Herald Publishing Association, 1953.

————— *The SDA Bible Commentary*. Vol. 4. Washington, DC: Review and Herald Publishing Association, 1955.

————— *The SDA Bible Commentary*. Vol. 5. Washington, DC: Review and Herald Publishing Association, 1956.

————— *The SDA Bible Commentary*. Vol. 6. Washington, DC: Review and Herald Publishing Association, 1956.

————— *The SDA Bible Commentary*. Vol. 7. Washington, DC: Review and Herald Publishing Association, 1957.

————— *Selected Messages*. Book 3. Washington, DC: Review and Herald Publishing Association, 1980.

————— *Testimonies for the Church*. Vol. 5. Mountain View, CA: Pacific Press Publishing Association, 1889.

————— *Testimonies for the Church*. Vol. 8. Mountain View, CA: Pacific Press Publishing Association, 1904.

————— *Testimonies on Sexual Behavior, Adultery, and Divorce*. Silver Spring, MD: Ellen G. White Estate, 1989.

———— *This Day with God*. Washington, DC: Review and Herald Publishing Association, 1979.

———— "The True Sheep Respond to the Voice of the Shepherd." *The Signs of the Times,* November 27, 1893.

We invite you to view the complete
selection of titles we publish at:

www.TEACHServices.com

Scan with your mobile
device to go directly
to our website.

Please write or e-mail us your praises, reactions, or
thoughts about this or any other book we publish at:

TEACH Services, Inc.
P U B L I S H I N G
www.TEACHServices.com ● (800) 367-1844

P.O. Box 954
Ringgold, GA 30736

info@TEACHServices.com

TEACH Services, Inc., titles may be purchased in bulk for
educational, business, fund-raising, or sales promotional use.
For information, please e-mail:

BulkSales@TEACHServices.com

Finally, if you are interested in seeing
your own book in print, please contact us at

publishing@TEACHServices.com

We would be happy to review your manuscript for free.

CPSIA information can be obtained
at www.ICGtesting.com
Printed in the USA
FFHW021916241118
49515734-53868FF